11-2-85

15-op

JESUS

MARTIN DIBELIUS

Jesus

Translated by
CHARLES B. HEDRICK
and
FREDERICK C. GRANT

Philadelphia
THE WESTMINSTER PRESS

PRINTED IN THE UNITED STATES OF AMERICA

FOREWORD

The name of Martin Dibelius, of the University of Heidelberg, is well known among Biblical scholars throughout the world. We in this country knew him, not only through his learned works in New Testament criticism and exegesis, but also as a result of his memorable visit in 1937 when he spent several weeks at our leading universities and theological seminaries. It was during this visit that he delivered the lectures on "The Sermon on the Mount," published in 1940. Many persons think of him chiefly in connection with Form Criticism; but he was equally eminent as an exegete, having published the famous commentary on The Epistle of James in the Meyer series (in 1920) and three volumes on other New Testament epistles in Lietzmann's *Handbuch*. In 1936 appeared his introduction to the New Testament, *A Fresh Approach to the New Testament and Early Christian Literature*. Several of his books on Form Criticism have also appeared in English: *From Tradition to Gospel* (1935); *Gospel Criticism and Christology* (1935); and *The Message of Jesus Christ* (1939). The present volume was published in 1939 in the *Sammlung Göschen*. Readers will find in this volume the same characteristic qualities that are found in all of Dr. Dibelius' work. He was not only a learned scholar; he was also a devout, earnest, Christian believer. His connection with the ecumenical movement and the World Council of Churches, his deep concern for theological education and for the whole life of the Christian Church, are well known. It was due to the tragic circumstances that led up to the war — as a non-Nazi he was constantly under the surveillance of the Gestapo — and to the tragedy of the war itself that his relations with Christian leaders in other lands were temporarily interrupted. His death on November 11, 1947, at the age of sixty-four, was undoubtedly hastened by the illness and privations caused by the war. Modern New Testament scholarship is far the richer by his having lived, far the poorer by his departure from us.

Charles Baker Hedrick was born in Palatka, Florida, January 31, 1877, and was educated at St. Paul's School, Concord; Trinity College, Hartford (1899); General Theological Seminary (1906); and Oxford University (1910–1911). Between college and seminary he taught for two years at St. Luke's School, Wayne, Pennsylvania; and between seminary and postgraduate study abroad he was rector of a parish in Starke, Florida. Returning home after his two years of study abroad (chiefly at Oxford, but also in Germany, where he met and married Hedwig von Bötticher, of Göttingen), he began his career as teacher of New Testament at Berkeley Divinity School (1911), then located at Middletown, Connecticut, now at New Haven. For thirty-two years he continued at Berkeley, until his death on January 12, 1943. His contributions to Biblical scholarship were chiefly articles, reviews, and chapters in joint works (e.g., the volume in honor of Professor C. F. Johnson, of Hartford, in 1928, and *The Beginnings of Our Religion,* in 1934). He was engaged upon this translation of Professor Dibelius' *Jesus* at the time of his death. His main field of interest was the Gospels, above all, the Fourth Gospel; and his whole life exemplified the spirit of the great Teacher at whose feet he continually sat. As was said of another saintly teacher, he never wrote a life of Christ — but lived it.

Since it was at my suggestion that Dr. Hedrick undertook the translation of this volume, I have felt it my duty to carry the work to completion. He left behind him a rough first draft, containing a number of alternative renderings of words and phrases. This draft went as far as the end of Chapter IX. I have revised this first draft and have completed the work, and I send it out now as a dual tribute to these two eminent Christian scholars and teachers of theology, the author and the translator, one a European and the other an American, both of them devout and learned Christian scholars. Before his death, Professor Dibelius kindly sent me the changes and additions for the second edition, and so the translation is up to date. I am confident that many students of the Bible, and many other readers as well, will find in this choice little book the quintessence of a soundly historical and at the same time a deeply religious understanding of our Lord and his mission.

F. C. G.

Union Theological Seminary
New York

CONTENTS

I

JESUS IN HISTORY

Christian faith, Christian doctrine, the Christian Church
— these tell us of Jesus. So also does world history — the history of the ancient East as well as of the Roman Empire, the
history of the Jewish religion as well as of the Christian. But
it is from very different standpoints that Jesus and Christianity are dealt with in the two cases.

Christian *faith* rests on the conviction that in Jesus God
has revealed himself. It is God who speaks in Jesus' words.
That these words are human must be admitted — all the
more so because we no longer possess them in their original
form, which was that of a Semitic speech strange to us. But
Christian theology is concerned not only with the meaning
of the Greek translation of his words that has preserved them
to us, but also with the import of these words as divine revelation. Moreover, it is also God who, according to Christian
faith, acts in Jesus' deeds. At the same time it must be recognized that we do not know all these deeds, and that even
those that have been reported to us we know only in the way
the believers of that day depicted them to their own age. But
Christian faith also declares that God revealed his will in the
passion and death of Jesus — nay, more, that God did not
leave him in death but exalted him to himself, " whence he
shall come to judge both the living and the dead." The fact

that at this point the accounts diverge from one another in part, and in part fade out altogether, shows only that faith is here abandoning the plane of earthly events and directing its attention solely to the action and purpose of God. Faith finds in this situation no embarrassment or refutation.

History regards Jesus from a entirely different point of view. On the border of the Roman Empire, in a small, inconsequential country of the East, and amongst a people of no importance in world politics, there appears a man with the announcement of an impending overturn of the world through the direct interposition of God. In God's name he addresses warnings, promises, and demands to his hearers; under God's commission he performs striking deeds, heals the sick, wins followers; he comes into conflict at the capital with the religious and political authorities and is executed. His followers, however, gather together in the faith that he has risen from the dead, has been exalted to God's side, and will shortly appear on earth in glory. This faith, in sundry variations and expansions, makes its way into the Roman Empire and wins a considerable portion of the human race — and of the Western portion, at that! Historical science is now occupied with answering the question, Why was it just this message, and not some other Oriental or Greek religious proclamation, that intervened so decisively in history, and determined the fate of whole races? But here criticism alone does not lead to the goal. The less credence one gives to the Christian records and the more one ranks Jesus' movement and message as one among many such in the history of the time, the more puzzling becomes this effect on world history!

The viewpoints of faith and of history cannot be simply combined. What is asserted by faith cannot be proved historically. Indeed, faith would not be faith if it could be demonstrated to every comer. Faith presupposes the decision to stake one's life — and one's death — on a message, a truth, a hope. Moreover, that message must be set above other, human messages; it must be regarded as revelation, as God's word. And just this definitive setting of the message above the context of general events is something that cannot be demanded of history. Although history not only affirms, but also evaluates, yet it can do so only within the frame of this general context. History can inquire why Christianity had such power to attract, and in what ways it excelled other cults. But history can never solve these questions by pointing to God. Faith, on the contrary, can be content with no other answer, be it what it may.

To be sure, scientific work and Christian faith can be combined in the same individual; otherwise this book would not have been written. But this individual has to see to it that certainties achieved through his faith are not mistaken by him for the findings of science, and, vice versa, that he does not give forth the "assured" results of his science as being for that reason saving truths. The scientific investigator has to pursue his critical task without looking at the result in advance. This does not mean, however, that he must be inwardly indifferent. One who is always indifferent never learns the great art of understanding. What is essential is often disclosed to faith — as it is also to the passionate rejection of Jesus: Nietzsche's criticism of Christianity is only an instance of the sharp-sightedness of enmity. There is no historical science absolutely devoid of presuppositions. The investigator's make-up and his own particular experience go into the shaping of every picture he draws. All he can do is to apply the critical technique of his science as conscientiously as possible and thereby re-present the past as honestly as he can. In the case of the life of Jesus he must make clear the

limited nature of our knowledge (see Chapter II); but he
must also do justice to the peculiar vitality of the tradition,
its great age and its relative unity.

For in spite of all the limitations to our knowledge it is not
a case of our having to forego a picture of Jesus or of having
to doubt even the historicity of his figure. To be sure, we
cannot describe the course of the events of this life except
during the last days. The communities that collected his sayings and the stories about him were interested neither in evo-
lution nor in psychology. They were much concerned, however, to preserve the words and deeds of Jesus, and in this
they succeeded in their own way, which is not ours. As early
as ten, or at any rate fifteen, years after Jesus' death, Paul,
like the other missionaries, came into possession of such traditions, oral or written. As early as forty years after Jesus'
death, books containing such collections existed in the communities. And the Gospel of John, unquestionably the latest of our four Gospels, was already being read in Egypt,
far from its land of origin, about ninety years after Jesus'
death — and a small fragment of such an Egyptian copy lies
today, in the original, in the John Rylands Library in Man-
chester! Thus all our four Gospels were in existence around
A.D. 100. Quotations in the Christian writers of the second
century show us also that there were still more such books;
that the accounts were being gradually expanded, in fact
disfigured, by the addition of extraneous ideas and stories,
but that a unified basic tradition was at hand. This whole
development is much clearer to us today than it was fifty
years ago. For this reason the periodically recurring notion
that the story of Jesus is only a myth — the story of a god —
transposed into human terms becomes more and more un-
tenable. For if that were the case, a reverse development
would have to be assumed — the second-century accounts

with their mythicizing tendencies would have to be assigned to the earliest stage and our Gospels of Mark and Luke to the latest.

Furthermore, the doubt as to whether our Gospels have been preserved in their original form turns out to be more and more unwarranted. To be sure, there are numerous deviations in the voluminous mass of copies; but it is a matter of ever fresh astonishment how unessential, on the whole, these "variants" are. That oldest fragment of the Gospel of John dating from the period 100–140 does not differ by a single word from our printed Greek texts. We possess carefully copied manuscripts of the Gospels from the third and fourth centuries on. The Greek and Latin classics, on the other hand, are known to us only from manuscripts that are separated by a considerably longer interval from the date of composition. No book of antiquity has come down to us in such old, such numerous, and such relatively uniform texts as the Gospels and the Pauline Epistles!

Thus, historical science need feel no misgivings about admitting the figure of Jesus into the sphere of its inquiries; the requisite foundations are there. Its task is to determine what we know of the historical phenomenon Jesus. In so doing it cannot demonstrate to faith what faith, and faith alone, is competent to say, but it can make clear to Christian believers and opponents alike just what is at issue between them — what it is that the one group exalts into being the guide of its life, and what it is that the other rejects personally or combats as a world influence. The importance which such knowledge of the historical reality has even for faith was stressed long ago by the Evangelist Luke when, in dedicating his book to Theophilus, he gave as his purpose in writing it, "That you may know the certainty of those things wherein you were instructed."

Alongside the Christian believers there stand today, more ominously than at any time since the first centuries, the *opponents* of Christianity. With them it is now no longer a question of contending against certain more or less incidental ideas or claims of Christianity. What they are assailing is the very essence of Christianity itself. The objective is not a reform of the Church but the extermination of Christianity altogether. This struggle, which will itself become history, cannot be decided by knowledge; there are stronger forces, in the last analysis, forces of "faith," which both sides have to bring into play. Christianity has no reason to shun this conflict; at the same time it cannot afford to belittle it in the eyes of its followers. The conflict has been in the air for some decades now. Its end will not be in our times.

The battle must be waged against the real foe, not against phantoms. Anyone who wants to make a clean sweep of Christianity cannot just attack little points of Church politics; he must envisage Christianity in its entirety, seeing it as a phenomenon of the past as well as of the present. He must take account of Reformation, medieval, and New Testament Christianity. It comes out, again and again, what a distorted picture of Christianity's beginnings has spread abroad. In the interest of faith, these beginnings have been lifted out of their historical context — even to the point of bringing their historicity into doubt. In the interest of general culture, men have discovered human greatness, perfect morality, wealth of feeling, and uniqueness of experience — all these have been found in the New Testament. But there are, we must admit, more "beautiful" books than the New Testament, there are more interesting books, there are even books that are more "moral" and more effective in calling forth emulation. The New Testament is both less and more. It is the simple, humanly conditioned deposit of an event. Whether in this event God made his will manifest — that is the crucial question at issue in the struggle over Christianity. A scientific presentation like the following cannot contain the answer but it can acquaint one with the event.

II

THE SOURCES

Our knowledge of the history of Jesus is limited. It is a limitation to start with that we have no direct report of the opinions of his opponents; for but little of the non-Christian testimony about Jesus has been preserved to us, and while that little is interesting, it adds nothing essential to the picture that we get from Christian sources (see § 1, below). Among the Christian sources the New Testament Gospels stand in the forefront; of the Christian reports of Jesus outside the Bible we have only fragments. The Gospels, however, are not literary works. Their authors are not giving independent portrayals of Jesus' doings based on personal experience and inquiry. They are not to be compared to biographies, either modern or ancient — and herein lies a further limitation of our knowledge (§ 2). Many questions that we should expect to find answered in a historical portrayal of Jesus are not dealt with at all in these books. The Gospel of John is, to be sure, an independent product, but its aim was not primarily to purvey historical information. The three other Gospels, however, are compilations of tradition — and, indeed, of essentially the same tradition, differing only in the way it is shaped up, arranged, and framed. This tradition contains sayings of Jesus and stories about him. And here a third limitation of our knowledge calls for mention. It consists in the fact that what we have here is

not consecutive narrative, but simply individual stories —
and these are told in the manner of the people — pious
people, who marvel at God's doings rather than ponder over
questions of purely human detail (§ 3). It is foreign to this
sort of narration to raise critical questions or to examine
whether or why this thing could have happened or that
thing could have been said. Our positive knowledge of Jesus'
history rests, therefore, on what the first communities handed
down from the life of their Master, and it is limited by the
special nature of this transmitted material.

1. The *non-Christian evidence* concerning Jesus ought
nevertheless to be mentioned here, because the question is
constantly arising as to whether it does not give us other and
better information about Jesus than do the Gospels. Of such
evidence the most famous — and justly so — is contained in
the *Annals* of Tacitus (xv.44), which were composed soon
after A.D. 110. Here Tacitus is telling how Nero met the
charge of having been himself responsible for the burning of
Rome. We read: " Now in order to put down the rumor,
Nero contrived to produce culprits to whom he meted out
the direst punishments; these were the people — detested
enough already because of all manner of abominable deeds
— whom the populace called ' Chrestians.' The name has to
do with one ' Christus,' whom the procurator Pontius Pilate
had caused to be executed during the reign of Tiberius. In
spite of being weakened for the moment the pernicious su-
perstition sprang up again, and that not only in Judea, where
this scourge originated, but also in Rome, whither everything
horrible and shameful pours in from all over the world and
finds a ready vogue." That element in these words which is
not just critical opinion (whether of the Christians or of

Rome) but rests back on history, Tacitus can easily have learned from any Roman Christian around the year 100. We have no need, therefore, to seek for special sources. They could not have been very good in any case, since Tacitus does not know the name " Jesus " at all and " Christ " he apparently takes for a proper name. The name was altered by the populace when they designated the followers of the Jewish prophet as " Chrestians "; this misunderstanding was quite natural under the circumstances because of the familiar name " Chrestus," and it is also attested elsewhere. If we can assume that the error was widespread, we then find Jesus mentioned by another Roman historian. In his work *The Lives of the Caesars,* written somewhat later than Tacitus' *Annals,* Suetonius relates (v.25.4) that " the Jews, who under the instigation of Chrestus were constantly creating disturbances, Claudius expelled from Rome." If this item really has anything to do with Christianity, it relates to disturbances that were caused by the intrusion of Christianity into the Jewish community at Rome. Suetonius would have heard the name " Christus " in this connection, construed it as " Chrestus," and then mistaken it as the designation of a Roman Jew.

Nor is much to be gained from Jewish sources. In his work called *The Antiquities of the Jews* (xx.9.1), the Jewish historian of this period, Josephus, mentions the stoning of " the brother of Jesus, the so-called Christ; James was his name." This mode of reference is not surprising. Josephus, who wrote at Rome around the year 90, must have known that the Christians' Saviour was called " Christos," as if this were a proper name; but for him, as a Jew, it was the translation of the title " Messiah," and therefore had to be qualified by the derogatory addition, " so-called." As soon as this guarded attitude of Josephus is understood, it becomes impossible to attribute to him the language in which the emergence of Jesus is described in another passage of the same work (xviii.3.3). For we read there, among other things, " This man was the Messiah [Greek, *Christos*] and on the third day he appeared to them alive again, which indeed, along with many other marvellous things, the divine prophets had said concerning him." Furthermore, when one reads at the beginning of the passage, " Jesus, a wise man, if he may be called man at all," hardly any doubt can remain that what we have here is a Christian interpolation, or at least a working over of the passage by a Christian hand. Just which it is, will always be a question. But for our purpose the decision is unimportant, for even if we were quite sure that in the original text of this passage Josephus had said something about Jesus, we still could not get back to his own words. We know only manuscripts with the full Christian-sounding text. There is, to be sure, a Slavonic version of Josephus' other historical work, *The Jewish War*, which also mentions Jesus in several places. But since the most important passage seems to be dependent on the Christian testimony just noted in the *Antiquities*, no historical information of an early kind is to be derived from this source, either.

Finally, there is still to be mentioned the great compendium of Jewish tradition that arose in the course of the centuries, the Talmud. This contains a few allusions to Jeshu ha-Notsri and his disciples, e.g., that he was hanged on the day of preparation for the Passover (Babylonian Talmud, *Tractate Sanhedrin* 43a). But since we have here only the last fading echoes of historical fact, to say nothing of distortions and perversions, the Talmud does not come into consideration as a source for the life of Jesus.

2. We are forced, then, to depend on the *Christian witnesses* to Jesus. Now there were, doubtless, more accounts of
Jesus' words and deeds than are contained in the New Testament. The Evangelist Luke, who did not yet know the Gospel of John, speaks of "many" predecessors, and he certainly does not mean by this only Matthew and Mark. And
even down to the most recent time fresh fragments keep
being discovered which contain collections of Jesus' sayings
or incidents from his life. Furthermore, in writings of the
Church Fathers, titles of other Gospels are mentioned, and
excerpts from them are quoted.[1] But what these "apocryphal" texts tell of the life of Jesus is often at variance with
the known conditions in Palestine; while at other times it
appears to be nothing more than interpretation or elaboration of what we have in the canonical Gospels. Their contribution in the way of sayings of Jesus is of more value. We
occasionally find a saying that in form and content is worthy
of a place alongside the canonical utterances of Jesus. More
important still, we find parallels to the latter which show
that Jesus' sayings were current in different forms. Comparison enables us now and then to fix the earliest form and the
original meaning of a saying.

Although the extra-Biblical material seldom enriches our
direct knowledge of Jesus, it does nevertheless afford us an
insight into the *history of the tradition.* The essential witnesses to this history are of course, regardless of all fresh
finds, the three oldest Gospels of the New Testament, those
bearing the names of Matthew, Mark, and Luke. What they
contain is substantially tradition of the same kind, i.e., stories
from Jesus' life, parables told by him, sayings and groups of

---

[1] Collected in German translation in Hennecke, *Neutestamentliche
Apokryphen,* 2d edition, pp. 1–110; in English, see M. R. James, *The Apocryphal New Testament,* pp. 1–227.

sayings in which he preached his Gospel, and at the close the Passion and Easter stories. And not only is their general character the same, but frequently the text of the individual units is so closely allied in the several Gospels that the differences are best understood as variations of a common type. This can be made evident by setting the texts of these Gospels in three columns side by side. In this way a common view or synopsis is obtained — a fact that has caused these Gospels to be spoken of as the Synoptics and their authors as the Synoptists. The kinship between them is explained therefore as due primarily to the fact that they are all three seeking to assemble the same tradition of the life and death of Jesus — the tradition that was preserved, either orally or in writing, in the Christian communities — and to give it in the form of an orderly and connected presentation. Their ways of doing this were different, but in no case had they the intention of creating something new, something peculiarly their own. That is, they were editors rather than authors. But this close resemblance of the three Synoptic Gospels to one another, not only in the character of the tradition but to a large extent in the text as well, is not to be explained solely by their partnership in a common stock of tradition. It appears that, somehow, these three Gospels are even more closely related to one another.

For a century and more, now, the criticism of the Gospels, especially in Germany and in Great Britain, has been engaged in defining this relationship. The result of this labor has been the so-called " Two-Document Theory," which in its main features is widely accepted today. By a minute comparison of the texts (especially those of Matthew and Mark) and by comparing the order of the separate units (especially as found in Luke and Mark), criticism has shown that the Gospel of Mark must have been the source of both the other two. Criticism has also made probable a second conclusion, viz., that Matthew and Luke used still another common source as well, for they agree almost word for word in many passages that do not occur in Mark at all. This source can be only approximately reconstructed from the parallel texts, but its contents, as thus arrived at, consist mainly of sayings of Jesus. How much else it contained, in what part of the Church it was read, to whom it was attributed — these are things we do not know. We now call it — but only since the beginning of this century — " Q " (= *Quelle,* " source "), in order to give it as innocuous a designation as possible.

The Gospel of Mark and the source Q are the most important formulations of the tradition that underlies the two longer Gospels, Matthew and Luke. Mark's contribution seems to have been more in the way of stories, Q's more in the way of sayings and collections of sayings, the so-called " discourses." We do not know what was the source of the rest of the matter contained in Matthew and Luke, e.g., certain sayings in the Sermon on the Mount and in the discourse against the Pharisees in Matthew, or several of the long parables in Luke. The tradition that was cherished in the Christian communities was certainly more extensive than what the Synoptic Gospels contain of it, and doubtless many a genuine bit survives — more or less distorted — only in the apocryphal Gospels, or — independently worked up — in the Gospel of John. In any case what we possess with most certainty from the ancient tradition is to be found in the Synoptics. They were written before the Gospel of John, who evidently knew them. This Gospel, which, as evidenced by that recently discovered bit of papyrus fragment from the first half of the second century, was already being read in Egypt at that time, is to be dated around the year 100. On the other hand, Matthew and Luke already take cognizance of the de-

struction of Jerusalem (Matt. 22:7; Luke 21:20). Thus the
rise of the Gospels, let us say, belongs in the last thirty years
of the first century; the tradition that underlies them must,
by the same token, be assigned to the period preceding.

It follows, then, that if we are inquiring about the sources
for our historical knowledge of Jesus we must try to reach
back and lay hold on this tradition. There is also the question of determining its nature and its worth. The significance of the Gospels lies in their being the mediums of this
tradition. Their individual peculiarities, the identity of their
authors, the question how far they are justified in bearing
their present names (Matthew, Mark, Luke) — these are all
subordinate considerations when it comes to the historical
treatment of Jesus' career.

3. We turn, therefore, to the *tradition* of Jesus as it stands
assembled in the Gospels. And first we must let it speak for
itself, and say what it has to tell us, especially about the conditions under which it arose. What we glean in this way we
can then compare with what we know of primitive Christianity from other sources, especially from the Pauline Epistles.

It is evident at the first glance that the tradition contained
both stories about Jesus and sayings of Jesus. Many a story
is only a saying fitted out in a narrative frame. A woman
pronounces a blessing upon Jesus' mother and receives back
from him the answer, " No, but instead, happy are those who
hear God's word and keep it " (Luke 11:27, 28). Or John the
Baptist sends messengers from his prison to ask whether
Jesus is the promised one or not, and Jesus, after pointing to
the signs of God's Kingdom taking place all about him,
closes with the warning, " But happy is he who makes no
mistake about me " (Matt. 11:2-6; Luke 7:18-23). In these

cases the answers are not to be understood without the questions; the sayings presuppose their frame. But many words
of Jesus have been handed down without any historical
frame; being intelligible by themselves, they became disen-
gaged from their historical context; and in this form they
come home to the reader even more directly than if they had
a narrative frame. That a need for this sort of tradition existed, and kept on being supplied even later, is shown by the
two papyrus leaves containing sayings of Jesus which were
published in 1897 and 1904 from the finds at Oxyrhynchus
in Egypt — the manuscript appears to date from the third
century. Here sayings of quite diverse content are strung together, but each is introduced, strikingly enough, with the
words, " Jesus says " (not " said "!). In the source Q, in its
Lucan and still more in its Matthaean form, these sayings are
frequently so linked together that whole " discourses " arise,
such, e.g., as the Sermon on the Mount. These are naturally
not original discourses; they do not take some one theme and
systematically develop it; on the contrary they are compilations of sayings and sayings-groups arranged according to
topics, showing that they were meant to supply the practical
need of the Christian communities — to provide answers to
their everyday problems and guidance direct from their Master's lips. This was the controlling motive in the collection
of the sayings of Jesus apart from their historical setting.

We obtain from these collections a very vivid impression
of the way in which Jesus spoke. He did not, like the Greek
philosophers, for example, take an idea and explore it by
means of a dialogue with a pupil or an opponent; nor did he
deliver little dissertations like a " lecturer." Rather, like the
prophets of the Old Testament, he proclaimed a message —
a message uttered in the name of God. In pronouncements
of salvation — such, e.g., are the Beatitudes — and in cries of

warning he charged and enjoined his hearers. Or again, like
a wisdom teacher, he set forth in short proverblike utterances,
often highly picturesque, God's claim on man and man's
position as regards God. These short aphorisms, appeals,
warnings, and commands are for the most part so vividly
and impressively formulated that we have no reason to be
surprised if they stuck in the minds of the hearers, later got
passed from one person to another in the primitive Christian
circle, and came in time to be written down without any
essential distortion. Since, however, Jesus spoke Aramaic,
though the tradition that has come down to us in the Gospels
is framed entirely in Greek, the words of Jesus must have
been *translated*. But since the earliest Christian communities
on the language frontier in northern Syria — in Antioch, for
example — contained many bilingual members, the translation will have been very easily effected through the simple
process of repeating in the one language what had been
heard in the other. Thus we are not to think of the translation as a single unified process like that underlying our modern translations of the Bible, but rather as a multiple process.
Indeed, there are actually instances of the same saying having come down to us in quite diverse dress. But it is just in
such cases of double tradition that we see how the form
varied without the content's being essentially disturbed. And
in other ways as well, we can see that Jesus' sayings were
handed down with great fidelity, thanks to the unencum-
bered memory of his unspoiled followers and to their reverence for their Master's word. Paul, and still more the Church
after him, already possessed other forms of expression and a
new thought world; if little or no trace of such usage is to
be found in the tradition of Jesus' words, this is the guarantee of the relative primitiveness in the tradition. It may well
be that, occasionally, similar sayings from other sources, espe-

cially from the proverbial wisdom of Judaism, have been added to the genuine sayings of Jesus; but they have not affected the essential content. It is proper to speak of non-genuine sayings only where the later circumstances, conditions, or problems of the already existing Church are clearly presupposed.

Jesus spoke in longer, interconnected utterances when, in parallel or repeated sayings, he applied the same admonition to different subjects, e.g., to almsgiving, prayer, and fasting (Matt. 6:2–6, 16–18), or to murder, divorce, and oaths (Matt. 5:21–37, although the passage has been filled out by the Evangelist with individual sayings). But the parallel structure of these " sayings-groups " affords such an aid to the memory — as anyone can test out even in our translated text — that here too a relatively faithful preservation of the text by memory seems quite possible.

Finally, there remain to be mentioned the longest pieces of connected discourse that have been handed down to us as sayings of Jesus: the *long narrative parables* — not those parables in which, in a few sentences, some incident, usually quite commonplace, is cited by way of illuminating a thought in the Gospel, but rather the detailed stories in which an incident, usually of an extraordinary kind, and sufficiently arresting in itself, is related in order to exemplify some item of the preaching or to throw light upon it from another sphere. It is the best known " parables " that come into consideration here: The Prodigal Son, The Laborers in the Vineyard, The Good Samaritan, the Unmerciful Servant, The Unjust Steward, Dives and Lazarus, the Talents (Pounds), The Great Supper. Most of these stories are distinguished by their popular motivation as well as by the popular stylization of the account (the three travelers in The Good Samaritan, the repetitions in The Laborers in the Vineyard, etc.). Narration of

this sort is so well fitted to imprint itself upon the mind and
the memory that there can be little doubt as to the accurate
preservation of these parables. To be sure, however, a comparison of the parables that have been preserved in two forms
(The Great Supper, The Talents) shows — and the same
thing is disclosed by an examination of the introductions
and conclusions of the singly attested parables — that in the
communities these parables were often overinterpreted, i.e.,
more was extracted from them than they were actually intended to convey. If what Jesus himself had depicted in The
Unjust Steward was a criminally minded but resolute man
who, after the collapse of his former mode of existence, built
up a new one (by fraudulent methods), there was nevertheless an attempt made later, as the addition in Luke 16:9–13
shows, to draw from it also a lesson on the right use of
money and property. The parable of the guests who rejected
the invitation to the great supper did not suffice as it stood.
It was reshaped in such a way that the fate of the Jewish
nation might be recognized in it (cf. Matt. 22:2–10 with the
simpler text of Luke 14:16–24). In general, however, these
interpretations and adaptations to later situations are easily
recognizable, since they usually stand in a strained relation
to the action and meaning of the parable itself. This meaning comes out most clearly when all enframing and explana-
tory comments are set aside and attention is confined entirely
to the text of the narrative. The fact that the text does permit
Jesus' meaning to be so clearly recognized, for the most part,
clearly indicates that he himself was but little concerned with
these amplifications and interpretations.

So far we have been dealing with the tradition of the sayings of Jesus, our aim being to deduce from the character of
this tradition how far those texts that were handed down
originally without any biographical context are historically

trustworthy and worthy to serve as sources for a historical
picture of Jesus. Minor alterations, such as were already involved in the translation from Aramaic into Greek, must also
be assumed, although they cannot be established in each individual case. Discussion as to whether a particular saying is
" genuine " is often idle because on neither side are the argu-
ments decisive. In general the historian will do well to look
at the tradition as a whole, and not build too much upon an
individual saying if it is at variance with the rest of the tradition.

More important alterations of Jesus' sayings by the communities can be established when the saying has to do with
Jesus' rank and fate. For the communities could not hand
on presentiments of Jesus' rank, and hints of his fate, without
giving expression to what they now knew, after the issue,
about Jesus' rank and now, thanks to the Easter faith, understood about Jesus' fate. This applies to such sayings as the
Passion predictions (Mark 8:31; 9:31; 10:32; and parallels),
which, lacking any connection, stand in the text only as
pieces of instruction without any special historical occasion.
But it applies also to sayings included in narratives, such as
Jesus' famous reply to Peter's confession of his Messiahship
in the form peculiar to Matthew (ch. 16:17–19). Finally it
applies also to the discourses of Jesus in the Gospel of John.
Since the Gospels are not biographies, but rather books aim-
ing to attest and confirm the Christian faith, the Evangelists
could not take over these sayings, supposing they had been
transmitted to them as presentiments and hints, without fill-
ing out the presentiment and stating the full faith in place
of the hint. The question is only whether any, and if so how
many, such sayings were actually transmitted to them. And
this question is for the most part insoluble along literary
lines. Behind it, however, stands the question how far Jesus

himself had already, in his own lifetime, turned his preaching into a proclamation about himself and his personal status. This question will be dealt with in its proper place (see Chapter VII).

We turn now to the *narrative sections* of the Synoptic Gospels. These too are not the creation of the Evangelists, but on the contrary have been taken over from the already existing oral, and eventually also written, tradition. Every reader, even of our translated text, can observe how, for example, the " narratives " contained in Mark, chs. 1 to 12, are completely self-contained units whose positions can be interchanged without affecting the picture of Jesus' activity. Only the Passion and Easter stories furnish an exception. Events in the main period of Jesus' ministry are known to us only from these isolated narratives. We are obliged therefore to forego chronological order from the outset, as well as the reconstruction of any development in Jesus, in his success, in his conflict with his enemies — a " biography " of Jesus in this sense cannot be written. All we know is individual incidents, not interconnected events. But these individual incidents are related at times with great animation. Any person attentive to such things soon notices a striking difference in the style of narration. There are narratives that say only what is absolutely necessary, but say this very clearly. A good example is furnished by the blessing of the little children, Mark 10:13–16, a narrative that is silent as to the scene, the persons who bring the children, or the grounds of the disciples' protests, but relates in unforgettable language Jesus' saying and Jesus' act. The much longer story of the paralytic, Mark 2:1–12, also belongs here: it is concerned solely with the combination of faith, forgiveness, and healing. But here there is no sparing of words: the odd approach by way of the roof attests the faith of the patient's carriers, the Pharisees contest Jesus' right to declare the forgiveness of sins, and the healing validates that right. But nothing is said about the patient and his feelings, or the precise nature of the illness or the manner of the cure. Over against this type there stands another, distinguished in the main by its abundance of detail, especially by the matters on which these details center. Here description of the illness, the act of healing, and the assurance of its completeness are the matters stressed. A good example is furnished by the lengthy story of the demon "Legion" (the Gadarene demoniac), Mark 5:1-17. There is a precise description of the man's behavior as a result of his possession, of how Jesus expelled the demon, and how the demon when expelled exhibited his power and legionlike character by "possessing" an entire herd of swine and driving them into the lake.

It is very instructive to observe both kinds of narration applied to the same theme. In the Gospel of Mark there are two stories of the healing of the blind. In one instance, in Jericho, Mark 10:46-52, it is the faith of the blind man and the command of Jesus that are described; the actual healing is disposed of in a single sentence. In the other instance, in Bethsaida, Mark 8:22-25, attention is focused entirely upon the cure that Jesus performs and upon the steps marking the man's gradual recovery. Of the "religious" aspects — of the patient's faith, for example — and of Jesus' power not a word is said.

This second manner of narrating is decidedly secular. And we know enough about popular narratives — for example, reports of healings outside Christianity — to be able to assert that this second style corresponds with the usual style there. But the style represented, on the other hand, by the blessing

of the little children, and the healing of the paralytic and of
the blind man at Jericho, is unique and is to be explained
only by reference to Christian presuppositions. This way of
telling about Jesus is obviously aimed at setting the power
of his word and the might of his deed in the foreground.
These narratives aim quite directly at proclaiming the Gospel. One can easily imagine that they were shaped in the first
instance to enrich, explain, or support the preaching of the
Christians, either missionary preaching or preaching at
home. They are brief enough — and at the same time sufficiently complete in themselves — to be inserted as examples
in a proclamation of the Christian faith. I therefore call them
"Paradigms." It is surprising to what a slight extent they
employ the otherwise customary means of popular narration,
and how little they serve to answer the questions raised by
our curiosity. They must therefore have acquired their basic
form at a time when the communities had hardly yet come
into contact with the Hellenistic world, that is, during the
first twenty to twenty-five years after Jesus' death. We arrive
at the same dating if we reflect that Paul himself had already
received such pieces of the community tradition as were
passed on to him, and that one of these pieces, that relating
to the Lord's Supper, I Cor. 11:23 ff., exhibits precisely the
type of narrative that we know from the Synoptic Gospels.
But these traditions must have come into Paul's hand when
he became a Christian (about A.D. 34) or when he became a
missionary (some years later). In these Paradigms, therefore,
we have before us very early tradition.

In this connection it is not very important for our problem
whether these stories were originally told in Aramaic and
later translated, or whether bilingual hearers, after listening
to the incidents in Aramaic, formed the accounts afresh in
Greek. In any case the Greek narratives arose at a period

when many eyewitnesses of Jesus' ministry were still living. They, especially the personal disciples of Jesus, would have been in a position to correct any egregious misrepresentation. Therefore in establishing the early date of these Paradigms we have also gained a guarantee of their relative historicity. To be sure, one can speak of this historicity only as relative, because these narratives have been stylized from the very beginning in order by their means to proclaim the Gospel story. They cannot and do not aim to be historically accurate accounts in the sense in which a modern official report is trustworthy in detail. What they seek to bring out in the occurrence is the action of the Son of God, and they may have attained this object, without the narrator's always being aware of it, by omitting the unessential, by overemphasizing the main points, by heightening the marvelous. And in general one has to remember that popular narration always works with methods of this sort and never corresponds to an official report. Conversely, if these stories were accurate accounts in the sense of modern historical writing, their origin would have to be placed at the earliest in the second century, the period when Christianity was becoming a concern of the cultured classes. Such as they are, with their excellences and defects, they point to an early origin.

The situation is somewhat different in the case of those more broadly executed stories of which the Gadarene demoniac and the blind man of Bethsaida have been cited as examples. They obviously do not serve the purposes of preaching. In their case narration, at times quite richly colored narration, is pursued for its own sake. Therefore it is no wonder that non-Christian influences are traceable here: either older stories have been supplied, in the course of transmission, with entertaining additions (in which case the substance would still be historical) or else non-Christian material has been attached to the person of Jesus (in which case there could be no talk of historicity). The historical trustworthiness of these stories, which I call " Tales " [*Novellen*] after their manner of narration, is therefore to be tested instance by instance, and certainty of judgment is not always attainable.

In addition to these Paradigms and Tales, as the sole instance in the Synoptic Gospels of a consecutively flowing account, there is the Passion narrative (Mark 14:1 to 16:8 and parallels). Here the narrator is led, by the very nature of the matter itself, to strive for a continuous account — all the more so because the Passion narrative has a peculiar place within the Gospel tradition as a whole. This is discernible most clearly in the speeches in the book of The Acts. When the preachers described there, Peter and Paul alike, speak of Jesus' life, they always refer to his Passion and resurrection, but his activity as healer and teacher is mentioned only now and then. Another evidence of the peculiarity of the Passion narrative is afforded by the Fourth Evangelist. Although elsewhere he goes his own way, when he comes to the story of the Passion of Jesus, he cannot, speaking by and large, tell it otherwise than as the other Evangelists have told it. It must accordingly be assumed that even in the earliest period there already existed a fixed model of the Passion story, which could be expanded but not departed from, because it had been handed down from the beginning. This general outline — as distinguished from the details — may therefore be viewed as trustworthy; even in the earliest period the story of how Jesus came to his death was being consistently told in the Christian communities. This happened at a time when numerous witnesses of these events were still alive — Paul makes direct reference to that fact in I Cor. 15:6 f.; indeed it is even probable that the oldest Passion narrative refers expressly in one or two places to such eyewitnesses: Mark 14:51, 15:21, and perhaps also 15:40 (see Chapter IX).

Upon what sources, then, can a historical knowledge of Jesus be based? They are, in the main, Christian sources — above all, the Gospels of Mark, Matthew, and Luke. But it is not primarily a question of what their authors knew and wrote down, but of older *traditional material* which they incorporated in their books. This material, partly oral, partly written, was already in circulation in the communities before the composition of the Gospels, and it consisted of narratives, sayings, and other bits of discourse (including the parables), and the Passion story. Since the Evangelists merely framed and combined these materials, the tradition can be lifted without difficulty out of the text of the Gospels.[1] The original is thus always the single unit of narrative, the single saying — not the connected text, the transitions, or the editorial notes which provide the continuity.

To distinguish the oldest layer in this tradition is therefore not hard, because we can trace the development that leads from the older layer to a later: the recasting of the narratives by the use of a secular style and of secular motifs, the adaptation of the words of Jesus to the later " situation," the reinterpretation of the parables. Whatever has escaped this treatment may be regarded as old. This older layer of the tradition we may take as relatively trustworthy, for the following reasons:

1. It arose in the period between A.D. 30 and A.D. 70, there-

---

[1] See the presentation of this material in German translation in Martin Dibelius, *Die Botschaft von Jesus Christus,* 1935; English translation by Frederick C. Grant, *The Message of Jesus Christ,* 1939.

fore if not through eyewitnesses at any rate not without some connection with them.

2. It is relatively free from extra-Christian influences; the sayings have neither a Gnostic nor a legalistic ring, the narratives do not yet exhibit the " secular " technique, the parables permit their original meaning to be recognized in spite of later " reinterpretation."

3. The brevity and pregnance of these pieces of tradition have the effect of imprinting themselves indelibly on the memory.

4. The oldest parts of the tradition are fitted, by their form, to be included in the sermon; in fact this relationship to the sermon has doubtless often conditioned their form. It is faith that speaks here, not research; and that is just what we ought to expect in the case of communities that were waiting for the end of the world. This means, of course, a certain curtailment of the historicity, but viewed as a whole it serves as its guarantee.

III

~~~~~~

PEOPLE, LAND, DESCENT

The people among whom Jesus worked were no longer
the Israelites of the Old Testament and not yet the Jews of
the Talmud. They were distinguished from the ancient Israel
by the lack of political independence. The small but vigorous
Israelitish people that had arisen out of the invading Hebrew
tribes and the indigenous Canaanites had led a now strong,
now weak, political existence only until 586 (or 597) B.C. —
until the conquest of Jerusalem and the removal of part of
the population to Babylon. Then followed the Exile and the
reorganization of the Jewish community under foreign sovereignty. In the second century the Maccabees, following the
revolt against the Syrian king Antiochus (IV) Epiphanes
and his Hellenizing policy, founded once more a relatively
independent monarchy; but quarrels over the succession and
the interference of the Romans — Pompey conquered Jerusalem in 63 B.C. — put an end to the existence of Judaism as
a state. The rule of the alien family of Herod was by the
grace of Rome. This holds good even of the so-called
"great" Herod, who in the struggle between Antony and
Octavian very shrewdly shifted to the side of the victor, the
future Caesar Augustus; it holds good all the more of his
sons, among whom Herod's kingdom was divided at his
death. The non-Jewish territory in northeastern Palestine
(eastward from the Lake of Gennesaret) went to Philip. The

northern province proper, Galilee, with a strip of East Jordan territory, went to Herod Antipas, who thus ruled over the region in which Jesus began and expanded his movement. Samaria and Judea, however, became the inheritance of Archelaus; after his removal (A.D. 6) they became Roman territory directly under a procurator. It was one of these procurators, Pontius Pilate (A.D. 26–36), who gave the order for Jesus' crucifixion. Thus the land in which Jesus worked, Galilee, and even more directly Judea, where he died, were ruled by a foreign power. When Jesus encountered the authority of the state, it was mostly foreigners who represented it; for even the auxiliary troops that were stationed in Palestine were not Jews. The local tax collectors, who obtained the concession by bidding for it, and had to exact for the chief tax collector as much as possible in indirect taxes — e.g., tolls on imported goods — were indeed Jews, but because of their dishonorable practices, and no doubt also because of their subservience to an alien government, they were so hated and despised that they were not counted as members of the Jewish community, and all intercourse with them was avoided. A Jewish court possessing civil and ecclesiastical authority was merely the " Chief Council," the Sanhedrin in Jerusalem.

But this peculiar political situation, resting partly upon the authority of the occupying power and partly upon the remains of indigenous authority, distinguished the Jewish people of Jesus' day also from the later Judaism which was driven from the country after the destruction of Jerusalem, and is presupposed in the great exposition of Jewish Law, the Talmud. The people in Palestine still occupied their own territory and continued to live by their own traditions; but for that very reason they were not obliged to cut themselves off so completely from the rest of the world as were the Jewish people later, when it became necessary for their self-preservation, exiled as they were from their land and scattered among the nations of the world. In *Judea* the Jewish population had kept itself relatively pure, but even there the influence of the Hellenistic world was to be detected: Roman coinage, a theater in the city of Jerusalem, and an amphitheater in the plain (after the time of Herod), as well as the rebuilding of the Temple carried out by Herod, presumably with features of Hellenistic architectural style, the military garrison in the Castle of Antonia north of the Temple area, the occasional presence of the procurator in the city — all these were a constant reminder of foreign domination and reflected the influence of the world outside.

Moreover, the great Diaspora, and the existence of Greek-speaking Jewries in the cities of the outside world, could not remain without effect upon the homeland. After the third century b.c. it was no longer Hebrew that was spoken in Palestine, but Aramaic. For the pilgrims and travelers returning from the Diaspora there were, however, Hellenistic synagogues in the capital; the official language of the procurators was Greek. Latin-Greek inscriptions are not wanting, and a knowledge of everyday Greek is accordingly to be assumed on the part of many Jews, not as a sign of special culture but as a necessity for business and professional life.

Thus even in Jerusalem one did not live cut off from the world empire and its culture, and that was all the more the case in the districts lying to the north, in Samaria and Galilee. In *Samaria* two cities, Samaria and Scythopolis, could be reckoned as predominantly heathen, since they had been settled by non-Jewish colonists. The inhabitants of the district of Samaria were, as regards religion, generally speaking, Jews, but, unlike the Galileans, they did not belong to the Jewish community, which considered the Temple in Jerusalem exclusively its own sanctuary. The Samaritans had their own temple, and after its destruction, in the second century B.C., their place of worship was on Mount Gerizim. Since they recognized only the five books of Moses, their manner of worship and their religious usages differed from those carried on in Jerusalem; but for all this they belonged to the sphere of the Jewish religion. To be sure, they did not belong to the Jewish race, or at least only in limited measure, since immediately following the conquest of Samaria, in the year 722 B.C., the Assyrians had settled foreign colonists in this province. A considerable part of the Israelite population had been carried off to Assyria; those that remained became in the course of the centuries more and more completely merged with the colonists. To the Judeans this mixed race, which, though it recognized the God of Israel, worshiped him in wrong ways, was an object of hatred and abhorrence.

In *Galilee* also there was a mixed population. In the northernmost portion, perhaps even before the destruction of Samaria, the pure Jews had not predominated. But after the Exile the Galileans had gravitated toward religious fellowship with the Judeans. For this reason they did not incur that hatred of the Judeans which fell upon the Samaritans. Furthermore, during the Maccabean period a portion of this mixed population in Galilee had been forcibly introduced (under Aristobulus, 104–103 B.C.) into the Jewish religious fellowship: the Galileans were circumcised and put under the obligations of the Law. It is a question if and to what extent this Judaizing process was assisted by the removal of Judeans to Galilee. In any case, the population of Galilee was thoroughly mixed, and was by no means purely Jewish; yet it was religiously attached to the Temple worship in Jerusalem, and in spite of minor differences the practice of the Law prevailed, just as in Judea.

In Matt. 26:73 the servants of the high priest say to Peter, "Your speech betrays you." That is an explanation of the

curious form in which Mark gives the words addressed to
Peter, " You also are a Galilean." And in fact one may recognize the Galilean by his speech. He does not distinguish the
guttural sounds clearly, he swallows syllables, and pronounces many of the vowels carelessly. And naturally a
much greater Greek influence is to be assumed in Galilee,
where the Jewish people bordered, so to speak, on the Hellenistic world, than in Judea. It is quite possible that Jesus
and his disciples understood Greek, perhaps even spoke it.

It was in this land of Galilee that Jesus was at home. In
the district along the Lake of Gennesaret, whose fertility and
mild climate the historian Josephus never ceases to praise in
some fresh form, Jesus carried on his ministry. It was in the
little town of Nazareth that he grew up. This town is entirely unmentioned in pre-Christian literature, though perhaps it is mentioned in a late Jewish song; its existence therefore does not rest on Christian invention. But was Jesus really
a Nazarene? Was he a Galilean?

The question of Jesus' origin, which is involved here, is
receiving more attention at the present time than formerly.
Back of it lies the further question, To which people and
race did Jesus belong? — and also the problem, Can Christianity be derived from the spirit of one particular race? Since
Houston Stewart Chamberlain's book, *The Foundations of
the Nineteenth Century* (1899), this question has not been
allowed to rest. History and anthropology are interested in
it and demand an answer from the Gospels — i.e., from writings that know nothing whatsoever about the question.
Hence it requires the most thorough consideration.

The Christian, who discerns in the words and in the coming of Jesus the revelation of God, is unwilling to account

for this revelation simply by the spirit of a race or a people. One's attitude toward Christianity, accordingly, does not depend upon a decision as to whether Jesus belonged to this or that race or people, but upon one's answer to the question, whether here actually — and, of course, in the midst of a people foreign to us — God was heard and apprehended. For that reason, on the other hand, no one, whether he be Christian or non-Christian, has a right to answer (and perhaps clear up) the historical question of Jesus' origin by reference to the worth of his message: by arguing that because the Sermon on the Mount and the Passion story have come to have significance for the entire Western world, Jesus could not have been of pure Jewish race! On the contrary, this question of Jesus' extraction can be dealt with only through the painstaking examination of historical evidence.

Here is what such an examination yields. As far back as the earliest tradition, Jesus is occasionally designated as son or descendant of David (Rom. 1:3; Mark 10:47). But what is in mind here is not so much a reference to kinship as a customary Messianic title. Jesus himself appears to have set little store by descent from David. He confronts the scribes with Ps. 110, " The Lord said unto my Lord," and asks them, obviously in order to make light of all genealogies of the Messiah, " If David himself calls him Lord, how is he then his son? " (Mark 12:37). It is quite possible, however, that certain circles of the primitive Christian community interested themselves in Jesus' origin and undertook to determine his pedigree, i.e., the ancestry of the carpenter Joseph. Two such tables of ancestry are given in the New Testament — in Matt. 1:2–16 and Luke 3:23–38. The first includes the official list of kings from David to Jechoniah; the second carries back Jesus' descent, by way of a side line, to David's son Nathan. These tables of ancestry remain in the Bible, al-

though the belief in the Virgin birth of Jesus renders the
ancestry of Joseph unimportant. Thus Joseph's (or Mary's?)
derivation from the family of David was maintained in many
Christian circles, and the story of Jesus' birth in Luke, ch. 2,
presupposes this derivation. The story of the Annunciation in
Luke 1:26–38 perhaps aimed originally to attribute Davidic
descent to the mother. Furthermore, the grandsons of Jude,
a brother of Jesus, are supposed to have declared in the reign
of Domitian that they were from David's family (Eusebius,
Church History, iii. 20). And since the Jews were careful
about preserving the tradition as to their ancestors, it is a
natural supposition that the family of Jesus also may have
had such information. But even if Jesus actually was of
Davidic descent, and the purpose of Mark 12:37 was in no
way opposed to kinship with David, Jesus' pure Jewish descent is not thereby assured nor a Galilean origin excluded.

According to the Gospels, Jesus lived in Nazareth until his
public appearance and was called a Nazarene or Nazoraean,
and in the Talmud "the *Notsri.*" In the case of the last two
terms it remains doubtful whether they have anything to do
with Nazareth at all or whether they are not intended rather
to express membership in a sect or a group. Nevertheless the
term "Nazoraean" is connected by the Evangelists with
Nazareth in Galilee. Jesus is regarded, therefore, as a Galilean.
Even if his family, regardless of whether it was of Davidic
origin or not, had settled in Galilee some generations earlier,
a doubt as to its pure Jewish character would still be permis-
sible. A doubt — nothing more; and besides, no certainty
would be attainable in that case as to what was the source
of the non-Jewish strain in its composition. The possibility of
non-Jewish ancestors must be acknowledged — but that is
all that conscientious examination of the tradition as to Jesus'
origin can find out.

There can be no doubt, however, that Jesus regarded himself as belonging to the Jewish community. The certainty
with which he quoted the Old Testament as God's revelation,
and the way in which, at the end of his ministry, he sought
a decision in Jerusalem, prove it. But in his case it is not
merely a matter of a so-called ecclesiastical membership. It is
something greater and stronger that he inherited from the
religious tradition of his people, something freed of all cultic
and legal framing or clothing, which furnished the presupposition of his own message. It is faith in the *reality and activity of God* and hope in *God's decision.*

The people of Israel had experienced the fact, and the Old
Testament, the Bible of Jesus, had preserved the experience,
that in the history of the people God had made known his
will, his severity as well as his love. Not knowledge of God's
nature, nor secret vision of his glory, was Israel's inheritance,
but the consciousness of having been summoned by God in
the Law, and of having been examined and tested by him
again and again in history. It is not an " all-loving Father "
that is proclaimed in the Old Testament, but the Lord of the
nations and the ages, who judges individuals as well as whole
peoples, who can reject as well as bless them, and whose Law
is the declaration of the divine will and the measure of human conduct.

This conception of God, very unphilosophical but directly
affecting mankind, had, of course, been enormously nar-
rowed in the centuries between Alexander the Great and the
advent of Jesus. The Lord of all peoples had become the
party leader of the legalists; obedience to the ruler of history
had become a finespun technique of piety. The nation no
longer stood in the midst of its own self-determined history,
and therefore no longer had any ear for the Lord who acts
through nations and upon nations. Among the populace it

was no longer the priestly nobility of Jerusalem that was most looked up to, but the group of the *Pharisees* scattered over the whole land, the " separated " (i.e., from all uncleanness?). They were the true champions of that technique of piety whose constant concern it was at every step of their life to fulfill some command and to violate none. They found their authority in the *scribes,* the inventors of that technique. Through interpretation of the Old Testament Law and application of it to the smallest everyday matters they developed a profuse tradition of precepts, which were handed down in the schools, and thus through the process of exposition and application became ever more and more numerous. These are the prescriptions which later, from the second century onward, in combination with other traditional material, were deposited in writing in the steadily growing collection known as the Talmud. By no means everything found in the Talmud can be claimed as evidence for Jesus' day; however, the Talmud does give a picture of the subdividing and compartmentalizing of life into legal cases, and of the accompanying restriction of the horizon, which already prevailed in Judaism in the time of Jesus. The great world, and indeed the political and social life of their own people with their tasks and problems, vanish from the sight of those who thus confine themselves to the study of the Law and to its application to the minutest spheres of human activity. The scribes did the first, and the Pharisees (among whom are to be reckoned many scribes) did the second; they formed a kind of brotherhood within the Jewish community.

In contrast to both groups stood that section of the populace who neither could nor would observe the Law — " people of the land " [*am ha-arets*] they are called in the Talmud. In specific contrast to the Pharisees stood also the professional defenders of what was ancient — the priests, and the group supporting them, principally from the priestly families, the *Sadducees*. Their name must have been derived from the personal name Zadok; perhaps the reference is to the priest of this name in the time of David (II Sam. 8:17). They did not share the faith in the resurrection and they rejected the Pharisaic elaboration of the Law. At least, the oral exposition of the Old Testament had no authority for the Sadducees; they were conservative in clinging to the written text of the Bible, conservative in guarding the Temple traditions, intent on maintaining the *status quo,* and therefore stood in fairly good relations with Herod and the Roman rule. The Pharisees, on the other hand, were closer to the simple folk, no doubt because they lived among them in the country. The Temple was far away, and the daily sacrifices were witnessed by the Galilean only when he visited Jerusalem on a pilgrimage. Close by, however, was the local synagogue — at once school and place of prayer — where every Sabbath he could worship God and hear the Law read, and come to know what he had to do and avoid doing in obedience to God.

With the mention of Pharisees, Sadducees, and "people of the land," however, the Jewish people at the time of Jesus are not fully described. Many a discovery has taught us that Judaism in Palestine exhibited more sects and parties than the historian Josephus would lead us to suspect. But even he mentions the group of out-and-out enemies of Rome, the *Zealots.* They were the Jewish "activists" who planned to employ revolution against foreign domination and sought to do so again and again, in minor revolts from the time of the death of Herod the Great, and especially from the beginning of the direct Roman rule in Judea, up to the great revolt of the year 66, the commencement of the Jewish War. It appears that the people in Galilee were especially open to revolutionary appeals, sometimes of a political, sometimes of a religious, sort: Judas of Gamala (east of the Sea of Galilee) was known as a leader of the Zealots; among the disciples of Jesus appeared a Simon the Zealot, apparently a former member of the revolutionary party converted to Jesus. And at the beginning of the Jewish War a Galilean bandit, John of Giscala, played a prominent role as a revolutionist.

But some decades earlier, even during the lifetime of Jesus, leaders of bands of robbers appeared again and again throughout the land. They seemed indeed to have aimed not only at gaining political power, but at the fulfillment of hopes such as were found in the Old Testament and in the writings that had appeared later, above all in the popular expectation connected with the person of the coming "Anointed One," the Messiah. Several of these leaders wanted to revive the kingdom: one promised a miraculous passage through the Jordan, another promised to overthrow the walls of Jerusalem by a miracle; prophets of good fortune and of ill increased their fame. Although the teachers of the people did not say much about the Messiah, and the authorities anxiously suppressed the Messianic hope, among the people this hope still survived. Anyone who came forward among these people with a promise and a claim to leadership at once stirred up the question whether he was himself the " Coming One " — or at least his forerunner, perhaps the Prophet Elijah, whose return was awaited as a sign of the Messianic age. These expectations and hopes were of different kinds. Those who saw in the Roman domination the root of evil may have thought more about an offshoot of David, who as king would restore prosperity to an empire of Israel. Those who bewailed the whole course of the world as opposed to God may have hoped that God would seize the rulership of the world from heaven, and realize his aims with his pious ones. Probably along with these hopes and expectations were combined those of other peoples and religions. For if the expected redeemer is also known as " the Man " or " the Son of Man " (which is the same thing), this was a reminder of the Persian expectation that the semidivine primal man would appear at the end of the ages. As early as The Book of Daniel (ch. 7:13), its author knew of this Son of Man who was to come on the clouds of heaven, though he saw in him an embodiment of the Jewish people; other such "apocalyptic" books, however, spoke of him as the world redeemer. The taking over of this title into the expectation of Jewish groups signified at any rate a new emphasis, not upon the political hopes of Israel, but upon the subjection of the entire world to God and his plans. But what is implied by the survival of all these hopes, native as well as foreign, is the consciousness of a tension between God and the present state of the world, the conviction that the Lord of the world would no longer allow this state to endure, the presentiment of a crisis, of an end of this present world age.

Unaffected by such eager expectations, the order of the *Essenes* led its quiet existence. This was a brotherhood which, shut off in settlements or even in cities, lived according to its own peculiar customs. Most prominent among these was a sacred meal of special kinds of food which the brothers ate, clad in holy garments, in perfect silence. Strict rites of purification, a worship of the sun, otherwise unheard of in Judaism, gave the fellowship of the Essenes its distinctive stamp. Their discipline separated them from the world: the renunciation or at least the limitation of marriage, the rejection of oaths, weapons, trade, and luxury were indicative of this. The presupposition of this common meal and of their life together and of their uniform white apparel was a form of communism, in which each one contributed his entire property and inheritance. Ascetic and moral obligations were something that Essenism shared with other brotherhoods; but on the other hand sun worship, food rites, and punctilious rules for purification appear to be peculiar to itself. Here one may trace influences of a non-Jewish kind; likewise the Essene doctrines of the soul and its immortality must be looked upon as foreign to Judaism.

Upon the life of the common people the Essenes had very little influence, and in the present connection there would be no occasion to say more about them were it not that by various writers Jesus' person and movement have repeatedly been brought into connection with the Essenes. The special knowledge of nature which is ascribed to them, probably rightly, is supposed to have made possible Jesus' miracles. The " Resurrection " rests back, according to this hypothesis, on the resuscitation of the apparently dead body of Jesus by Essene physicians, who because of their white clothing were taken for angels. Then one may also point with justice to the kinship of certain strict commands, e.g., the forbidding of oaths, both among the Essenes and among Jesus' disciples, while the silence of the New Testament regarding the Essenes can be explained as deliberate secrecy. All such attempts, however, are contradicted by the plain fact that nothing that we know about Jesus points toward Essenism; while some of the things recorded by the New Testament sources make the Essene hypothesis absolutely impossible. In fact there was lacking in the appearance of Jesus everything that would have been considered as typically Essene: we hear neither of sun worship nor of holy garments nor of a secret meal (the Lord's Supper is something entirely different). We do hear, however, that Jesus more than once violated the Jewish Sabbath law — and the Essenes were regarded as especially strict Sabbath observers. We read of Jesus' attitude of disregard for the Jewish regulations about cleansing — and the Essenes outdid other Jews in such strictness. Finally, Jesus was derided as "a glutton and a wine-bibber" (Matt. 11:19) — while the Essenes were strict ascetics.

There were other groups among the Jewish people who belong with far greater right than the Essenes to the antecedents of the movement led by Jesus; such, for example, were those who were waiting for "the Man" who was to come from heaven, or Galilean adherents of the Messianic faith, or pietistic religionists of one sort or another. In order to decide such questions one must first of all know whether the nickname of Jesus found in the Talmud, "the *Notsri*," and also the Biblical name "Nazoraean" are really connected with Nazareth or refer to some other geographical designation or to the name of a sect.

Quite certainly, however, the circle that gathered about Jesus stood in close relation with one of the groups that regarded an immersion bath, i.e., a "baptism," as a sacred sign which distinguished them from others. For this group, and for their leader, this sign was a mark of preparation for the coming world transformation which their leader proclaimed. It was John the Baptist who came forward with this message — and with him the story of Jesus begins.

IV

~~~~~~

THE MOVEMENT AMONG THE MASSES

The oldest tradition of the Christian community, as characterized on pp. 23 ff., begins with the appearance of John the Baptist. Of events in Jesus' youth only one is reported, and this only in one Gospel: it is the familiar story of the twelve-year-old Jesus in the Temple (Luke 2:41–51). Accordingly, it by no means belonged to the traditional material familiar to all the communities. And of the birth of Jesus two Gospels, Mark and John, know nothing, while the other two have very different accounts to give. Thus these stories are likewise not to be reckoned as part of what the first preachers of the message reported. They began with the baptism movement of John. This was the "beginning of the gospel" (Mark 1:1).

According to some Bible passages (Matt. 11:12; Acts 1:22; 10:37), not only was the Baptist regarded as the forerunner of Jesus, but his movement was also regarded as the dividing line between the old and the new age. This is the reason why Luke (ch. 3:1, 2) opens the account of Jesus' work with a chronological notice on the appearance of the Baptist. This passage affords an important point of reference for the *chronology* of the life of Jesus. One is not to look for any absolute certainty in this matter. Like many points of time in ancient history, the dates in Jesus' life are not ascertainable

with absolute exactitude. Especially must it be borne in mind
that in dealing with this life we are not dealing with an
" official " event; that there were no inscriptions, no chroni-
cles, probably also no Roman court record which would have
contained a dated report of Jesus' life. Finally it must be emphasized that we cannot figure out the length either of the
Baptist movement or of Jesus' activity. The oldest tradition
does not by any means consist of a consecutive account; it
is made up of single narratives and single sayings (see p.
29), and they can give us no information as to the length
of time within which the things reported took place. If one
often speaks of Jesus' ministry as covering two or three years,
this reckoning rests on the mention of three Passovers in the
Gospel of John (chs. 2:13; 6:4; 11:55). But it is very questionable whether in these passages the Evangelist meant to
indicate a chronology. He arranges his material according to
other points of view. The cleansing of the Temple he puts at
the beginning instead of at the end of Jesus' ministry, and
in his way of writing he might quite well have mentioned
the same Passover several times. The other Evangelists mention only the Passover celebration at which or before which
Jesus died. But even so they have not affirmed a ministry of
only one year. It might well be that another Passover, or
even several, fell in this period; the old stories would mention it only provided some act or other of Jesus' was connected with the festival.

When one takes all this into consideration, it must seem
surprising that we still know as much as we do about the
chronology of the life of Jesus, and especially that we can fix
inside relatively narrow limits the time within which all that
the Evangelists tell of Jesus' ministry took place. The life
of Jesus stands within fixed historical contexts. It did not
take place in remote antiquity, like the deeds of mythical

heroes. Neither does it hang suspended in some indefinite period, as is the case with Siegfried, King Arthur, Doctor Faustus, and other figures of legendary lore. There are, in fact, an array of witnesses who permit us to insert Jesus' ministry into a relatively closely defined period:

1. According to all the ancient sources, Jesus was executed by order of the Procurator Pontius Pilate; according to Luke 3:1, 2, the Baptist also appeared under Pontius Pilate. Now according to Josephus, Pilate held office for ten years, which according to Josephus' data must be fixed as A.D. 26–36 or 27–37.

2. According to Luke 3:1, 2, John the Baptist appeared on the scene in the fifteenth year of Tiberius. As the Evangelist Luke always has an eye for the connection with secular history, one may credit him in this case with drawing upon an official computation, i.e., of reckoning from the time when Tiberius actually became emperor and not including the years (A.D. 12–14) when he reigned jointly with Augustus. It was customary at that time to count the period before the next New Year, in Syria until October 1, as the first year of a reign; and the question is only whether the date is to be reckoned from the death of Augustus (August 19 in the year 14) or from the moment when Tiberius actually took office, perhaps not earlier than the month of October in that year. In the former case the first year of Tiberius would extend only to October 1, A.D. 14, in the latter to October 1, A.D. 15. The fifteenth year would, in the former case, have to be taken as A.D. 27/28, in the latter as 28/29.

3. According to all the Gospels, Jesus was crucified on a Friday in the Passover season. According to the oldest Gospels, this would have been the first Friday of the Passover. John, however, assumes a tradition (e.g., ch. 18:28) according to which the Passover meal did not take place until after

the Crucifixion, so that the first day of the feast fell on the following day, the Sabbath. There is much to be said for this dating (see pp. 128 f.). If anyone accepts this date, he must look for a year in which the Sabbath and the first Passover day coincide. This, according to astronomical reckoning, was twice the case in those years, on April 7, A.D. 30, and on April 3, A.D. 33 (the days of the month according to the Julian calendar).

But this reckoning is burdened with still another uncertainty, apart from the question whether the data in the Gospel of John reflect the correct chronology. The Jewish Passover began on the fifteenth of the month Nisan; but the beginning of the month was determined in those days by popular observation of the new moon and not by astronomical calculation. Moreover, an intercalary month may have been inserted before the month Nisan on grounds of agricultural necessity. It is questionable, therefore, whether the fifteenth of Nisan as reckoned according to the astronomically correct new moon coincided with the fifteenth of Nisan as actually observed.

4. An inscription enables us to determine a date in Paul's life fairly accurately. According to a letter of the Emperor Claudius to the inhabitants of Delphi, preserved in an inscription there, Gallio, the brother of the philosopher Seneca, was proconsul of Achaia in the year 51/52 or 52/53. His entrance into office in the summer of 51 or spring of 52 gave the Jews in Corinth the wished-for opportunity (according to Acts 18:12) to bring a charge against Paul, who (according to Acts 18:11) had already labored there for eighteen months. Therefore, Paul's arrival in Corinth must have been at the beginning or the end of the year 50, and the meeting of the apostles in Jerusalem described in Gal., ch. 2, and Acts, ch. 15, had probably taken place in 49 (or 50). Accord-

ing to Gal. 1:18 and 2:1, Paul had been a Christian at that
time for three plus fourteen years, i.e., perhaps for fifteen
or sixteen years, since it was the custom at that time to include the initial year. The conversion of Paul thus took place
between the years 33 and 35.

One may therefore say with considerable certainty that
Jesus died between 27 and 34, probably in the year 30 or 33.
The appearance of the Baptist falls in the period between 27
and 29. It is seldom that events which like these occurred off
the main highways of the world's history can be dated
within such a closely marked out period. It is remarkable
with what confidence we can make the following affirmation: Within the range of at most seven years there took place
in the politically insignificant land of Palestine, and unno-
ticed by the political and spiritual leaders of the day, events
that have set the world moving in an entirely new direction.

These events began with the *baptism movement.* In the
Jordan steppe, on the reed- and shrub-covered floor of the
valley which extends along both sides of the Jordan throughout the southern part of its course, a hermit, John by name,
carried on his lonely existence. Like the Prophet Elijah, he
was clothed with a pelt, which was held together by a leather
girdle; his food was what he found in the steppe. In dress
and in diet he thus seemed like a living protest against the
civilized life of the people in the towns and villages, and
especially against the Hellenized culture of the court. Such a
hermit existence, to which in time disciples also bound themselves and pursued a similar way of life, was by no means
unique in those days. New, however, and strange, was the
preaching of this man and his practice of baptism.

He proclaimed to his disciples, and to the crowds that

came flocking to the Jordan to hear him, that the "fulfilling" of the times was drawing near. The Day of the Lord was at hand, on which a judgment would be held — of the godly as well as the ungodly. The one who is to exercise the judge's office, and separate the chaff from the wheat, is to be the Fulfiller, the Greater One whose shoe's latchet he, John, is not worthy to unloose. For those who live face to face with this day of wrath, John knows only this one way of escape: Repent and be baptized!

Repent — in John's mouth that signifies no ritual performance and no ascetic discipline, but the holy dread that overtakes the unholy in the presence of the holy God, and the turning of one's whole life toward God. The baptism is not the ritual bath that was required of every heathen converted to Judaism, and of every Jew who had become unclean by contact with something heathen. It was, instead, something new and unheard of — otherwise John would not be called the "Baptist"; it was something connected with his own person — otherwise one would not have had himself "baptized by him." Its purport is easily stated: one who has himself baptized expects to "escape the coming wrath." But the baptism is no magical performance, for it promises escape only to the seriously repentant; at the same time it is no merely symbolical act in the modern sense; it is rather a "sign" in the antique meaning of the word, which guarantees the mysterious union of the symbolical act, now occurring, with the future event which the symbolical act prophesies.

Much more difficult to answer is the question as to the origin of this baptismal bath. It was not Jewish, as has already been said. In the country east of the Jordan there seems to have been more than a single baptismal brotherhood; and the sect of the Mandaeans still living today in

Baghdad and along the Euphrates — a sect which has called itself the John-Nazoraeans — may well be a lost remnant of such a group of Baptists. It may be that it was from a setting of this kind that John took over the custom of the baptismal bath, in order of course to give it a new meaning, one relating to the coming world transformation. It was not a mere act of cleansing; the Jewish historian Josephus, who understands it in this way, is in error at this point, just as he is in making completely innocuous the Baptist and the Baptist movement in general. Indeed, as far as that goes, there is remarkably little said in the New Testament about any cleansing effect of baptism, but a striking amount, on the other hand, about its relation to dying and being born again (Mark 10:38; Luke 12:50; John 3:5; Rom. 6:4; Col. 2:12; Titus 3:5; I Peter 3:21). In such ideas may lie the ancient meaning of the baptismal bath, which gave John the Baptist a right to employ it in connection with his preaching about the coming judgment: a voluntary and therefore precautionary forestalling of the great catastrophe which God had determined shortly to bring upon the world. If the Evangelists speak of a " baptism of repentance for the forgiveness of sins," it is because they reflect the Christian rather than the Baptist feeling.

Among the many who flocked from the towns and villages of Palestine to the Jordan Valley to have themselves baptized came Jesus from Nazareth in Galilee. This connection of Jesus with the Baptist movement is an authentic fact; no Christian would have invented it. Jesus thereby affirmed what he certified later through his praise of the Baptist as the greatest of all those born of women, viz., that in John's call to repentance and in his command to be baptized God had spoken to the nation. Whether Jesus himself received or discovered his mission at the moment of his baptism, as is implied in the Christian story of the heavenly voice, is something we do not know. Everything that the Evangelists tell us about the inner life of Jesus originates in Christian interpretation and understanding of the events, not in auto-biographic confessions of the Master (for the latter would have been handed down in direct discourse, if they had ever existed). We know with certainty only this: the Baptist movement was taken by Jesus as the sign that God's Kingdom was in fact drawing near.

The imprisonment of the Baptist seems to have been for Jesus a second sign, a command to begin his own ministry. From this event Mark dates the preaching of the Gospel in Galilee, Jesus' own movement. The Baptist fell into the power of the tetrarch Herod Antipas, who ruled not only over Galilee but also over the east side of the Jordan. Mark relates that John criticized the tetrarch's second marriage. Josephus gives us to understand that other motives also played a part; in spite of the innocuous cast he gives to the Baptist movement, the Jewish historian is obliged to ac-knowledge that Herod Antipas regarded the Baptist as po-litically dangerous. In fact, a preaching that gives rise to the expectation that the Messiah will come tomorrow or the day after portends danger for those who are now in power — and so it is no wonder that the Baptist was finally executed in a fortress in the territory east of the Jordan.

But Jesus had already taken the decisive step in the mat-ter of his own activity. He had returned to his Galilean homeland, perhaps already accompanied by disciples; ac-cording to the indications of the Fourth Gospel, several of Jesus' disciples had earlier been among John's closest follow-ers. The gathering of an inner circle of disciples belongs to the work of Jesus as it did to the Baptist's movement. Com-mon also to Jesus and John is the keynote of their preaching:

The time is fulfilled; repent, for the Kingdom of God is near!

Equally clear, likewise, are the things that distinguish the Galilean preacher from the Jordan baptizer. The scene of their activity is striking, to start with. As an ascetic removed from the world, John dwelt in the steppe; as judge, arbitrator, counselor, or physician, Jesus frequents the towns and villages in immediate contact with the people. From the Jordan Valley came a cry that aroused the country to repentance; the message of Jesus is gentler but more urgent, for it says to each man just what he must now do. Still more important, all that John had to give as the sole consequence of his call to repentance was the direction to be baptized; one who is baptized is now waiting for the coming Kingdom. But Jesus is already able to communicate to others in word and deed the powers of God's Kingdom; one who is taught or healed by him is already within the Kingdom.

For this is the content of the *new movement,* which Jesus inaugurates on his home soil: he arouses the people by the preaching of the Kingdom, but at the same time he lets them detect in the wrath of judgment, in the word of counsel, in the act of healing, the nearness of the Kingdom — a nearness that meant both bane and blessing. Thus he travels from place to place surrounded by his group of disciples. But in the places that he touches he leaves behind a larger circle of adherents — people who remain in their families and at their work, but are nevertheless ready to testify to Jesus' cause, to lodge the Master and his followers, to follow his instructions and warnings.

The command of poverty, the watchword to "follow" Jesus on his journeyings, holds good only for the inner group of *disciples;* it states the presuppositions of their existence; it says nothing about moral duty as having any value by itself. This is implied by the fact that the disciples are twelve in number, a figure that equates them with the twelve tribes of which the nation originally consisted. The number is symbolic; in reality there are more traveling companions than this. The names of disciples in the Gospels exceed the limit of the figure twelve; several women, and perhaps still others (Acts 1:21), belong to the list. Only in the case of a few do we know how Jesus gained them. The first to be called by him, the brothers Simon (with the nickname " Cephas " or " Peter " — both meaning " rock ") and Andrew, fishermen from the Lake of Galilee, are associated with the promise, " I will make you fishers of men " (Mark 1:17). Here too the oldest tradition is silent about the psychological circumstances; whether they already knew Jesus, whether he talked with them at length, is not stated. Only a later narrative (Luke 5:1-11) permits us to see (perhaps with historical correctness) that the saying about fishers of men was spoken in connection with a miraculous draught of fishes. The Gospel of John tells of a disciple Nathanael, whom Jesus persuaded by clairvoyant knowledge regarding an event in his life — this is implied in John 1:48 rather than explicitly stated. To another, however, who sought to go along with him, but only after he had buried his father, he called out: " Follow me, and let the dead bury their own dead " — not as if Jesus' message forbade the fulfilling of the obligations of filial reverence, but because the decision for the Kingdom of God cannot be postponed (Matt. 8:22). The transition from the obligations of the wider circle of followers to the demands on the immediate disciples is effected by the well-known story of the rich man who wanted to attain eternal life. Jesus seeks to admit him into the familiar circle — " You know the commandments " — and only when he asserts that he has fulfilled these is he given the startling com-

mand to sell his possessions and give the proceeds to the
poor. This is not a regulation applying to everyone, but is
God's demand on this particular man and at this particular
hour — a demand that exceeded his powers (Mark 10:
17–22).

For most of the inner circle of followers of Jesus the step
from ordinary life to an itinerant one was not attended with
such great sacrifices. For what they gave up was the poor and
narrow life of fishermen, farmers, craftsmen, or publicans.
What they got in exchange was an equally poor but free life
of constant journeying. Its poverty was not a practice of asceticism, but was the condition of their participation in this
movement inaugurated by Jesus. Its features were preaching
in the open air, in houses, in synagogues, the healing of the
sick, and constant journeying — then repetition of the same
activity in another place, and so on through Galilee and the
neighboring regions.

In general, Jesus directed his attention to people of Jewish
faith, members of the synagogue communities — that they
were, of course, race-pure Jews cannot be asserted in regard
to Galilee, as has been shown (pp. 39 f.). When Jesus crossed
the boundaries of Galilee, he had heathen people before him;
but he also encountered them elsewhere. Occasionally heathen individuals sought his help, such as the centurion in
Capernaum and the Phoenician woman in the neighborhood
of Tyre. He fulfills their requests, but expressly emphasizes
each time that his mission is directed only toward Israel. The
new people of God are to be gathered out of the old and prepared for the coming Kingdom. It is Jesus' death that first
opens the way for " the many," and it is the exalted Lord who
first wins the world — so at least primitive Christianity, if not
Jesus himself, regarded his work (Mark 10:45; 14:24; John
12:23). Thus it was understood that Jesus himself, apart

from exceptional cases, had remained within the national boundaries of Judaism.

The disciples were his helpers; they were even collaborators in his work. Sayings have been preserved that order them to go forth to preach; and although these, especially as found in Matthew (ch. 10:5), seem to have been recast into an instruction for the primitive Christian missionaries, it nevertheless does not follow that all such sayings arose at a later time; it is evident that from the time of Jesus' journeys the disciples also proclaimed the approach of the Kingdom of God. Cures are demanded from the disciples, to be sure, but not accomplished (Mark 9:18); the new beneficent powers of the coming Kingdom are bound up with the person of the Master.

A movement of an eschatological and Messianic kind in Galilee, distinguished above others by special gifts of its Leader and by the absoluteness of the motives and hopes aroused by it — this, but nothing more than this, is what Jesus' ministry in Galilee appears to have been. It may occasionally pass beyond the border districts and encroach on foreign territory; a methodically arranged and thoroughly prosecuted mission among the heathen does not take place, for Jesus does not set out to gain the non-Jews. Popular favor may turn toward him or away from him: the thronging of the masses does not become a real danger for the Jewish and Roman authorities, nor does the falling away of the disappointed become a threat of revolt against the Master. The fate of the Baptist may also be in preparation for him — but a political misconstruction of the message of the Baptist seems to have been much more readily possible than of the Gospel of Jesus. For the Baptist worked in the vicinity of the political and religious center of the country, Jesus in the remote North. Anyone who wishes to ascribe political motives to Jesus will find no foothold in his Galilean activity. A political movement would have had to struggle against the rulers, and would have been hunted down by Herod. Above all it would have had to seize the most important and most modern city of Galilee, Tiberias on the Lake of Gennesaret, which by its name testified to the renown of the emperor and, with its court life, to the renown of the tetrarch. But Jesus appears to have avoided Tiberias. The central point of his journeys is Capernaum, and neither the choice of this place nor his sojourn in other neighborhoods can be construed as signs of a political tendency.

The only journey of Jesus' whose goal is recorded and whose purpose can be deduced is the journey to Jerusalem at the end of his ministry. The Galilean prophet and holy man, well known among his nearer countrymen, decides to seek out the capital of the country, the city whose character is determined by the priestly nobility, by Pharisaism, and by the Roman garrison. Here is the center of worship; here the Pharisees play a special role; from here, it is hoped, the Kingdom of God will take its start. We do not need to engage in psychological speculations; the meaning of this journey is clear without that. In Jerusalem the new movement will present itself to the authorities of the country; in Jerusalem the ultimate verdict must be pronounced; in Jerusalem the hopes of the Kingdom of God will be realized.

Whether Jesus was often in Jerusalem we do not know. The Gospel of John describes several visits in the capital city, but it has chosen the scenes of action more for their symbolical significance than for their chronological sequence. Jesus' saying of Jerusalem, "How often would I have gathered your children together" (Luke 13:34), may be a quotation, but it may also refer to the decisive visit to Jerusalem at the close of his life. In any case Jesus has not heretofore sought or demanded a decision in the capital, nor asserted the ancient hopes and claims in the way he does now with his entry into the city and his action in the Temple. He means not only to be heard there — he means to be either accepted or rejected by men there; and he means to confront the capital with the message of the Kingdom of God.

All this may be concluded from the fact that Jesus took his followers with him to Jerusalem. It is the one and only indication known to us of a development in the history of Jesus. The movement that Jesus set going in Galilee was transferred by this change of scene to the religious center of the country. Thereby, so it appears, it was brought to the bar of decision. In reality, however, looked at from the viewpoint of world history, what stands at the bar is not Jesus' circle but rather Judaism itself. The reasons for and the conditions of this outcome can be made clear only after we have discussed the content of the movement herein depicted. What we perceive from without does not yet explain the outcome of Jesus' ministry; and especially it does not account for the fact that this outcome was not an end but a beginning, the fact that the movement of Jesus lived on in the Church of Christ.

V

THE KINGDOM OF GOD

"Blessed are ye poor, for yours is the Kingdom of God!"
"Thy Kingdom come!" "Howbeit, seek ye his Kingdom,
and these things shall be added unto you!" "Fear not, little
flock, for it is your Father's good pleasure to give you the
Kingdom!" At the center of Jesus' message stands the Kingdom of God. Anyone who wishes to understand the Gospel
must know what sort of thing this Kingdom is.

Several psalms begin with the exclamation, "Yahweh is
king" (Ps. 93; 97; 99); others describe his ascending the
throne (Ps. 47; 96). In this way, in ritual observance or in
prophetic vision, the future is anticipated — that time when
the God of Israel will finally seize the reins of government,
and when his sacred justice will prevail upon earth. For as
yet discord and unrighteousness rule; as yet the world's
course does not run in accordance with the law of God; as
yet the devout sigh in misery and desolation. But when God
seizes the rule, then it will be made known by revolutions in
nature and history; his enemies will feel it with horror, his
faithful with rejoicing that God's sovereignty has arrived
at last.

This rule of God in the last days is what is meant when
the Jew speaks of God's reign. There is no thought of a section of territory in the world that has been marked off for
God; the place of his rulership is the whole cosmos. Neither

is there any thought of a hidden sway of God in the soul of man; rather, God will come forth "out of his dwelling place" in power and rule in manifest glory. One prays therefore that his Kingdom may "appear." And yet the expression "Kingdom of God" can well become the designation for God's cause, to which the devout man confesses allegiance even now, because he knows that it will be realized in splendor in the future. Abraham, even in his day, it is said, chose God's Kingdom; and the heathen who becomes a proselyte (that is, goes over to Judaism) takes upon himself God's Kingdom. And when Judaism came, later on, to have a confessional formula which was said daily — beginning with, "Hear, O Israel," from Deut. 6:4 — this repetition of the formula was called "taking upon oneself the yoke of the Kingdom of Heaven."

The expression "Kingdom of Heaven" does not differ at all in meaning from "Kingdom of God." From an early time there was among the Jews an aversion to pronouncing the divine name. They spoke of the Kingdom of "the Lord" instead of the Kingdom of "Yahweh," but they said "Heaven" instead of "Lord" — the later Judaism was even accustomed to speak in a quite colorless way of the "Place" or the "Name" when there was occasion to speak of God. So it is to be understood that one said "Kingship of Heaven" when one meant God's Kingship, God's Kingdom. Those Christian communities in which Jewish ways of speaking persisted kept these forms of expression, and thus they found entrance into Matthew's Gospel. But Matthew himself says "Kingdom of God" in several places (chs. 6:33 and 12:28), where the phrase is required for rhetorical balance — and therefore we may assume that Jesus himself spoke in the main of the Kingdom of God.

In those days, anyone who referred to "the Kingdom of

God " implied thereby that this present world is not God's world. It was out of an experience of a world order that exalts the godless and humbles the devout, punishes the guiltless and lets sinners achieve honor — it was out of this that the longing for God's Kingship was born. A time would come, so it was announced, in which this evil course of the world would be turned about to its opposite, when right would again be recognized as right and sin as sin. This wonderful change could not be wrested from Heaven by men, nor could it be accomplished by their effort; all that men could do was to be prepared for the universal change. However, when it does come to pass, the whole world will be able to recognize it. When the coming Kingdom of God appears, there will be an end to all questioning. The only questions for study or inquiry are: When will it come? and, Is it perhaps already near at hand? Until it actually appears, the Kingdom of God will always be viewed as a coming kingdom. So John the Baptist viewed it, and so also Jesus views it.

Any attempt to interpret the individual sayings of Jesus about the Kingdom must be preceded by a recognition of the fact that *Jesus never specifically interpreted the expression " Kingdom of God."* He at no time said anything like, " You have heard that it was said to them of old time, the Kingdom of God will come; but I say to you, the Kingdom of God is already here." He spoke of the coming of the Kingdom, for which one should pray. It is God who sends it. Jesus said neither that it grows gradually nor that he meant to create it.

Of course there are several parables that seem to speak of the growth of the Kingdom of God. But if one keeps to the viewpoint expounded on pp. 26 ff., and reads the parable narrative apart from its editorial frame, then one will understand what it is these teaching stories are meant to say. The point of Mark 4:26, for example, is that the situation with regard to the Kingdom of God is like that of a farmer who has sown seed, but after that has nothing more that he can do; nay, the earth brings forth of itself blade and ear and fruit. Only when the fruit is ripe is it time again for the farmer to take a hand, since now the harvest is here. It is the introduction, especially, that one must be careful not to misunderstand. As we must infer from Jewish parables generally, this introduction does not signify a logical comparison, but simply serves as a heading: such is the situation with regard to the Kingdom of God. But the picture that this little teaching story sketches has one clear, simple meaning. It affirms that one can do nothing: the harvest comes of itself. It does not affirm, however, that the harvest is already here. Nor does it affirm that the Kingdom of God is like a grain of seed that becomes fruit by a process of self-development. For the thing being compared is not the fruit, but the harvest. The parable is an injunction to wait, not an exhortation to sow.

And likewise the oft-cited parable of the Sower (Mark 4:3 ff.) does not develop a theory about the Kingdom. It portrays the partial failure with which all seed-sowing is attended: some seed falls on the path, some on the rocky ground, some among thorns. It is only by way of appendix that there is any mention of the many seeds that fall on the good ground, i.e., the parable is intended to afford consolation for the failure which lies in the natural course of things and a standing reminder of the success in the work of seed-sowing. The point is not that one can disseminate the Kingdom; not one of Jesus' hearers could have entertained this utterly impious thought. The reference embodied in the picture is not open to any doubt: it is the preaching of Jesus (and of his disciples) about the Kingdom of God. This preaching is not to be bewailed as fruitless because much of it is a failure; failure is the accompaniment of every success.

The figures of the Mustard Seed and the Leaven (Mark 4:31, 32; Matt. 13:33) likewise have no other purpose than to console and encourage. They show forth only how what is large comes from what is small, in the case of the mustard seed through growth, in the case of the leaven through human effort. But such a thing is possible, and the small beginning is no indication of what the final result will be. Of course it is not said as general truth, but with reference to the Kingdom of God; hence the question, "How shall we liken the Kingdom of God?" But in this case also no hearer of Jesus understood that the Kingdom was going to grow, naturally or through human effort. What is small at the beginning and becomes large at the end is the *preaching* of the Kingdom of God, the cause for which Jesus is concerned.

This preaching is not, however, the teaching of a prophet who foretells that one day, at the end of the ages, the Kingdom of God will appear. What aroused Jesus' hearers and inspired the disciples is the special, the "actual," viewpoint under which the preaching of the Kingdom stands: it is the message that the fullness of the times has *now* drawn near, that the Kingdom of God is standing before the door, that its coming is not to be delayed. And now we recall that this certainty links the Baptist with Jesus. His preaching likewise proclaimed this "now," the absolutely imminent invasion of the Kingdom of God. Until then, the Kingdom lives only in the preaching and in the movement of the people affected by this preaching. And in Jesus' circle this nearness is traced to his words, his decisions, his deeds. The Kingdom has not yet appeared, but its *signs* are visible. The old world still exists, with its enmity toward God and his Kingship; the heralds of the Kingdom still face hostility; their message is still denied and despised by the mighty who control this world — and under that heading men of the ancient world did not think only or primarily of Pilate and Herod, but of supernatural " powers," concerning which the Apostle Paul also wrote more than once (I Cor. 2:8; 15:24; Col. 2:15). In such a connection, Jesus' saying also becomes easy to understand — a saying that has often been styled a dark saying: " From the days of the Baptist until now the Kingdom of God suffers violence, and men of violence seek to take it by force " (Matt. 11:12). But that has held good only " until now " — for " it is your Father's good pleasure to give you the Kingdom " (Luke 12:32).

One can understand Jesus' mission only if he keeps in view these two poles between which lies everything that he said and did. The one pole consists of the conviction that the Kingdom of God is future and completely opposed to this world. The other consists of the consciousness that this Kingdom is already in process of coming, and has already put itself in motion; its breaking in upon the present order is no longer to be held off. The movement among the people which Jesus set going advances from the time of unfulfillment into that of complete fulfillment; but it exists in the period between these times. This existence between " not yet having arrived " and " having arrived " one must understand if one is to comprehend the historical position of the Gospel. With this as a starting point one can find the answer to certain much discussed questions, such as: What historically did Jesus aim to do? or, Did he " aim " to do anything at all? or such a question as this: What did he think about his own person?

But of course there arises, precisely out of this recognition of an existence between the times, a great question, one that touches and gathers up the whole mission of Jesus. The Kingdom of God has not yet come; we are still living today " between the times " and are still confronted with the " not yet."

Here one cannot speak merely of a widening of the horizon, in the sense that the still unrealized fulfillment has only been postponed a few hundreds or thousands of years. It still looks as though a monstrous illusion lies at the basis of the whole mission of Jesus, the illusion of something immediately impending which actually never has come to pass. These fundamental questions will be discussed later (Chapter X). For the present we must leave them unanswered; we can come to grips with these superhistorical questions only after we have dealt with the historical situation, and have learned what this existence "between the times" was actually like, in the Palestine of those days. Only with a full knowledge of the historical picture can we speak of its validity or invalidity in the course of the centuries and also in our own time. Only when we see what Jesus brought to his own time in the way of *threat, promise,* and *demand* are we justified in asking if this threat, promise, and demand apply to us also.

The threat stands first in this connection. For the coming of the Kingdom of God signifies judgment, destruction of the present world order, and the end of this world age. The nearness of the holy God always signifies danger for the unholy man. Jesus does not speak of the Kingdom of God as though it were an idyl. He takes God really seriously as the One who is to come and to judge. What will happen when he suddenly enters into this world?

> " Two men will be working in the field:
>   One shall be taken, the other shall be left.
> Two women will be grinding at the mill:
>   One shall be taken, the other shall be left "
>   (Matt. 24:40, 41).

And as in the days of Noah men will not notice anything; they will eat and drink, marry and be given in marriage —

and as then the flood came and suddenly destroyed them all, so shall the judgment come upon them now. The suddenness of the catastrophe Jesus depicted in ever fresh figures: its appearing will be like the lightning, which shines from the east even to the west; or like the thief, who slips into the house at an hour that no one knows; or like the lord who returns in the night without the servants' knowing it (blessed are the servants whom he finds watching!); or like the bridegroom who suddenly surprises the waiting virgins (woe to those who are unprepared, who have no oil for their lamps!).

Many Jews believed they were prepared. They had their books, ostensibly of miraculous origin, the "revelations" (apocalypses) in which they found written what should come to pass. Here too there were not lacking pictures that suggested the nearness of the end: "Near is the jug to the spring, and the ship to the harbor, and the caravan to the city, and life to death" (Syriac *Apocalypse of Baruch.* 85). But now come calculations as to what must take place before the end: that, e.g., four kingdoms must pass away, or twelve plagues must come upon mankind, and monsters rise up out of the sea. Sun and moon will be darkened, stars will fall from heaven; there will be uprisings among the nations, and discord among princes; wars between various countries will terrify men — these are the signs according to which pious curiosity reckoned the time of the end.

The Christian community likewise felt the need for such a calendar of events. Accordingly some Christian undertook to furnish Jesus' words of warning and promise regarding the catastrophe with "apocalyptic" motives in order that the Christians too might be able to note the course of things and recognize the "signs" of the end. And this brief Christian "apocalypse," which was widespread in the communities, was taken up in time into the tradition of Jesus, since it did indeed contain familiar words of the Master. In this way it

found a place in our Gospels as a " discourse " of Jesus concerning the end, and there it is still to be read today, in the
thirteenth chapter of Mark's Gospel and in the corresponding passages in Matthew and Luke. That this is not really a
discourse delivered by Jesus is especially easy to discover from
the Marcan text, at the point where a mysterious expression
is taken over from The Book of Daniel: " But when you
see the abomination of desolation standing where it [or he]
ought not, then let the inhabitants of Judea flee to the moun-
tains " (Mark 13:14). This saying, which foreshadows the
worst — a pernicious something, which works desolation,
shall stand in a holy place — is provided in Mark with the
addition: " Let the reader understand." Thus it has nothing
at all to do with hearers of Jesus, but on the contrary with
readers who in conformity to their Christian experience are
to apply the ancient symbol of calamity to an event of their
own time, which will then become for them the predicted
sign of the end. By the time Luke wrote, the correct " understanding " was believed to have been arrived at. For Luke
replaces the suggestive word with a reference to its fulfillment: " But when you see Jerusalem encompassed by armies,
then know that its ' desolation ' is near " (Luke 21:20).

One can understand how the Christians, especially those
in Palestine, were at pains to understand in such fashion the
disturbed times before and during the Jewish rebellion, and
to insist on the point. But when they too began to reckon
with " signs," they ceased to act in accordance with Jesus'
mind. His opposition to such apocalyptic methods is only
too clear. If men were as God would have them be, they
would know how to interpret " the time," just as one recognizes in the clouds the coming rain and in the fig tree's
leaves the nearing summer. There is no doubt (and they
should have been able to observe it) that the time is ripe: the

man who stands before them witnessing by word and deed to the Kingdom of God, the band of disciples which he is gathering, the movement of the people which is spreading throughout the land — all this should have opened their eyes. Just as Jonah became a sign for the inhabitants of Nineveh, so *Jesus himself* is the sign of God's Kingdom. The Christians also tried to get out of this saying another positive sign, and later compared the Prophet Jonah's emergence from the belly of the whale with the emergence of Jesus from the grave (Matt. 12:40); but the form of the Jonah saying in Luke (ch. 11:29, 30) and the rejection of all quest for signs in Mark (ch. 8:12) leave no doubt as to Jesus' meaning: Jonah brought the people of Nineveh none of those predicted apocalyptic signs, but rather he himself, his call to repentance, was the one and only signal that was given them. If one fails to understand that, he cannot complain; God will not perform a special miracle for him, wherewith he may bemuse himself.

Indeed, the contemporaries must have noted already in the gloomy " preacher in the wilderness," in John the Baptist, that here " the way of the Lord " was being prepared. They could also have learned from the Law and Prophets what were God's purposes for the course of this world. In such a sense Jesus retold the story of the rich man and poor Lazarus, which, as we know, was already in circulation before his time: the rich man in Hades, anxious about the future fate of his brothers, can send them no hint, no special sign, for " they have Moses and the prophets " (Luke 16:29). But if one really senses what is breaking in over the world, he will also be well aware that he is on the way to judgment, and he will act like a clever peasant who meets his adversary on the way, before they arrive at court, and quickly, while they are both walking into the city, comes to terms with him —

for when once they have appeared before the judge it will be too late. This saying, also, the Christians expounded further in their effort to produce as many of Jesus' instructions as possible for individual situations in their own life: they understood it as an exhortation of Jesus to the amicable settlement of lawsuits (Matt. 5:25). But the introduction in Luke 12:57 shows that the saying is a parable: " Why do you not let your own life teach you the right attitude? " — i.e., Why when you are on the way to God's judgment do you not act in the same clever way that you do on the way to a human judge?

Recognition of the time, not a reckoning of the times, that is what Jesus demanded of his hearers. And one should recall how many among his people relied upon such spiritual arithmetic! Only then can we understand in what sense he said (Luke 17:20), " The Kingdom of God comes not with observation [the art of reading signs]," i.e., there are no signs to be observed that give notice of it. The second sentence explains the first with the parallel thought: " Neither shall they say [of the Kingdom], Lo here! or, There! " But at this point Jesus now adds the often quoted, often misunderstood sentence, " For lo, the Kingdom of God is among you "; one can also translate, " in you." This saying, in the form of the second rendering, is frequently construed as the basic principle of pure inwardness: Jesus sought to do away with all hope for a coming of God's Kingdom from heaven on earth, and to affirm that the so-called Kingdom of God is in reality only to be found " inwardly present within you," in the souls of believing men. But how many words of Jesus' would have to be put out of commission if this should hold good! Any such reference to pure inwardness is also refuted by the opening sentence. For without doubt what is " among you " (or " in you ") is just this and nothing else, viz., something that men might readily " observe " and of which they might say in their excitement, " It is here," or " It is there "; what is meant therefore is not the Kingdom itself but the signs of the Kingdom. They are not to be " observed," let us say, in the starry sky, nor are they to be confirmed by any sensation-greedy excitement " here " or " there." The signs of the Kingdom are " among you " or " in your midst "; they are Jesus, his message, his deeds. The translation " within you " is excluded on objective grounds, for Jesus' message is not yet alive in the hearts of his contemporaries, but he does stand before them as the sole yet definitive " sign."

"No trace of God's Kingdom shall they find, who seek it by reckoning,
Nor any trace of it shall they find who say, 'It is here,' or, 'There.'
For behold, God's Kingdom is to be found in your midst! "

VI

~~~~~~

THE SIGNS OF THE KINGDOM

Those who sought in the star-studded sky or in the great events of the time for signs that pointed to the end of the world and the beginning of God's Kingdom could easily pass Jesus by; what was expected among the Jewish people as the sign of the Coming One was not fulfilled through Jesus. "No sign shall be given!" So the words ring from his lips — or what comes to the same thing: "No sign other than the sign of Jonah." But that saying about the Kingdom of God which is "among you" gives us to understand that for Jesus there is only *one* sign of the Kingdom: his own person, his preaching, his movement. It is not so important what one calls him if only one understands this sign and perceives in Jesus' activity the coming Kingdom of God.

That Jesus wanted to be so regarded is shown by the extremely important tradition of the *sending of the Baptist's disciples* to him. John the Baptist had heard of Jesus while in prison; the prisoner's communication with the outer world, so it seems, was not entirely interrupted, but was maintained through visits of his disciples. But John could not arrive at certainty as to whether this Galilean prophet was really the promised Anointed of the Lord, the Messiah; whether he was the One whose coming he, the Baptist, had once proclaimed. Was he really the Greater One whose shoe's latchet John did not feel himself worthy to unloose?

Was he the Judge, who separates the chaff from the wheat and casts it into the unquenchable fire (Matt. 3:12)?

John had no personal experience of the significance of Jesus. If the Gospel of John makes him a witness of the appearance of the Spirit at Jesus' baptism (ch. 1:32), that is because the Christian account of this appearance transfers to the Baptist an experience of the one baptized; in this way John's Gospel, but only John's, makes a Christian of the Baptist. If the Gospel of Matthew represents the Baptist as at first declining to administer the baptism because he feels himself unworthy (ch. 3:14), that is simply a later Christian solution of the problem that the baptism and the apparent subordination of Jesus to the Baptist presented to the communities. Luke and Mark know nothing of such a conversation. Jesus' appearance in no way corresponded to the picture of the Messianic Judge of the world as envisaged by John. It is quite understandable that the Baptist did not know what he ought to think of Jesus. So through his disciples he addressed himself to Jesus: " Are you yourself the Coming One, or must we wait for another? "

Jesus answered him neither " Yes " nor " No," but only pointed to what was taking place round about him. And he did it in words that would evoke in the hearer the picture of the coming Kingdom of God, words that perhaps, if we may draw an inference from the poetic style, belonged to a Messianic hymn:

> " The blind see and the lame walk,
> The lepers are healed and the deaf hear,
> The dead are raised,
> And the poor receive the message of salvation."

As to himself Jesus added only this: " Blessed is he who is not offended in me! " (Matt. 11:2–6). It is not assumed that

all those marvels have actually taken place in the presence
of the messengers; but things of this kind are known to have
happened, and those who have experienced them must see
in them the manifestation of the powers of the Kingdom
in their midst, as God's proclamation announcing its coming. Anyone who perceives what is happening in Jesus' presence will believe! He will not be misled by the fact that Jesus
himself does not show the traits of the traditional picture of
the Messiah; whatever one may call him, the Kingdom is
in process of coming, that is certain!

The same implication is to be found in another saying
of Jesus, one applying to events of a similar sort, i.e., those
cures that were looked on in that day as the expulsion of
demons who had taken up their lodgment in sick persons.
This saying may have been uttered in connection with a
controversial debate. The devil's exorciser has been suspected
of being in league with the devil: he casts out the demons
by means of the archdemon Beelzebul, their chief.[1] But
Jesus retorts to his calumniators that Jews also drive out demons: "By what power then do your people drive them
out?" And he adds, "But if it is by the finger of God that I
expel the evil spirits, then God's Kingdom has already made
its presence known among you" (Luke 11:19, 20). In this
saying too, whose wording permits the translation, "God's
Kingdom has come even to you," it is not said that God's
Kingdom is already there — of such a statement, these expulsions taken alone would really have been no proof! — but
that in the abundance of such wonderful events it announced

---

[1] Mark 3:22. The ancient translations were the first to change this
word, which means "lord of dung" or "lord of the dwelling," into
Beelzebub, "lord of flies." See II Kings 1:2; Beelzebul must be the name
of a demon, perhaps in purposely perverted form.

its proximity. Hence the demon expulsions are also signs of the coming Kingdom.

Thus from Jesus' own words we discover the consciousness that he is performing mighty works of this kind and that these works announce the nearness of the Kingdom of God. God is already beginning to transform the curse of this present existence, which appears in sicknesses and other dark fatalities, into blessing. The populace have perceived this in the fact that here more is happening, and of a different sort, than in the circle of the Baptist. It was remembered that the latter had done no signs (John 10:41); all the more significant, therefore, appeared what Jesus was accomplishing before the eyes of all. The extraordinary acts that are told of Jesus are accordingly not something that was imposed on his portrait later on; from the beginning they formed an essential part of the tradition about him. Jesus moved through the land not only as a preacher of the Kingdom and a judge of men, but also as their benefactor, who, with his special "charismatic" (i.e., God-given) gift of healing, practically demonstrated to many persons the nearness of God's Kingdom. It is these acts that the language of everyday calls "miracles." And before we ask how this tradition that Jesus performed such signs is related to the other fact already noted in the preceding chapter, that he looked upon himself as a God-given sign, we must devote some consideration to these miracles and to the current opinion of them.

When one speaks of Jesus' "miracles," one ordinarily means deeds that appear to transcend normal human capacity and to contradict our (certainly still incomplete) knowledge of nature's laws. Of course the New Testament, when it mentions "signs" or "mighty works," does not have in mind that negative notion of the contradiction of nature's laws, but something very positive, viz., that in these deeds God himself is acting, that they are evidences of Jesus' close bond with God and of the nearness of God's Kingdom. There are persons to whom Jesus means so much, and the conception of the world disseminated by natural science means so little, that they see no problem here — who never ask the question, What really happened? and who need no explanation, but instead uncritically take what they read in the Gospels for the thing that occurred. For them, of course, there is really no need of going into further explanations, either as to what happened or as to how it came to be reported as it is.

And yet it must be said that the attitude of all of us toward a miracle, including even that of the uncritical, is quite different from that of Jesus' contemporaries (and from that of the medieval man as well). We have become accustomed, and even feel it our duty, as far as we really take faith in God seriously, to recognize God's activity in normally explainable events, indeed chiefly in such. But Jesus' hearers, none of whom had been seriously influenced by the critical philosophy of the Greeks, supposed that God's working was to be seen precisely in the inexplicable. If something inexplicable should happen in our world and before our eyes, if someone should cause a person who was lying dead suddenly to get up perfectly well, or if a man should lift himself up into the air without using any mechanical means to help him, the stouthearted would regard the event as a subject for investigation, the timorous would draw away from it, those who disapproved would call in the police, while the enthusiastic would give the news to the press — but nobody, we can be sure, would fall on his knees in prayer! But this is just what seemed to Jesus' hearers the most natural thing to do when confronted by the marvelous. To them, anything that was not instantly explicable was miraculous. They did not reckon with laws of nature or trouble themselves with attempts at explanation, for it was the supernatural that they sensed at once in the unexplained. It was a case for either adoration or condemnation, for seeing either God's hand or the devil's at work — there was no other alternative, for them. We, however, insist on first having the unusual explained before we pass judgment. On the other hand, the happenings in nature that are known to everybody, a human birth or death, the renewal of vegetation in spring, the unison rhythm of a great mass gathering, or the grandeur of a work of art — these often enough prompt us to worship or thanksgiving, and out of such experiences of shock or exaltation there arises, confirmed and renewed, faith in the God who is at work there — but openly, not in the dark. " Miracle is faith's dearest child " — that holds good perhaps for the uncritical man of the bygone and even of the present day, but in no case for the faith that endeavors to hear God's voice in the events of everyday. Just for that reason we — in harmony with our own religious situation — bring scientific considerations to bear on the " miracles " of Jesus.

The tradition that Jesus performed extraordinary deeds is as well guaranteed as such a fact can be guaranteed at all by means of popular reports. But alongside this positive judgment must immediately be placed a critical one: none of these reports is at pains to give a clarifying presentation, none of them inquires about the medical diagnosis of an illness or the factors entering into the cure. These narratives do not set out to explain, but to transfigure, to exalt; their purpose is to make God's power visible, and not the human circumstances. It has been shown already (pp. 29 ff.) that two types of narrative style can be distinguished in the Gospels, which achieve this purpose in differing ways: one simply, but in a genuinely primitive fashion (the "Paradigms"); the other in greater fullness, but with motives that are also employed outside of Judaism and Christianity in such narratives (the "Tales"). None of these accounts narrates without any purpose whatsoever; only, in our attempt to find out what really happened, we must begin with that type which seems least influenced by other literatures, i.e., with the Paradigms.

Now this type of narrative shows with utmost clearness that it would be a mistake to reject the whole report as unhistorical. For we see precisely in these short and, in the literary sense, unpretentious narratives that Jesus' healing activity stands in the service of his whole message about the Kingdom of God. With the healing often goes an announcement: he heals the lame man in order to demonstrate the legitimacy and the genuineness of the forgiveness of sins pronounced by him; the man with the withered hand in order to unmask the rigid Jewish Sabbath observance in all its mercilessness. The story of the centurion of Capernaum is told to bring out the confidence of the heathen centurion in the supernatural power of Jesus' command; the cure of the "possessed" in the synagogue at Capernaum justifies by means of an act what Jesus has previously announced in this synagogue. What is certain in the case of the "possessed" is probable in other cases of illness: we have to do with psychically conditioned maladies which are healed by means of an impact upon the psychical life of the patient. And this impact is effected frequently by means of a command which brings about a psychical reaction: "Arise, take up your bed and go home!" Such curative commands are also known to modern medicine. Use has been made of them in cases of lameness caused by war, e.g., as the result of pressure on a nerve or something similar, and we now speak of a therapy by means of sudden inspiration [*Überwältigungstherapie*]. That emotional states such as fear or anger have curative effects was something the ancients also experienced. An inscription from the sanctuary of Asclepius in Epidaurus tells about a lame man by the name of Nicanor. A boy stole his indispensable crutch from him, but he sprang up and pursued the thief — and so was healed. In the case of Jesus' cures, one must think of entirely different and quite special psychical factors. The oldest accounts do not tell of a miracle worker, who performs as many miracles as possible, but of the proclaimer and guarantor of the coming Kingdom of God; God himself is drawing near to the world, and his nearness is perceived in the fact that through Jesus he speaks, through him he acts, through him he heals.

Those reports which are modeled upon the pattern of the Tale occasionally present Jesus as one of the ancient miracle workers. They tell about the sickness, how long it has lasted; about the means Jesus employed in the cure, for example, the laying on of hands, or the utterance of a formula, or even the use of spittle; and finally the evidence of success: the girl restored to life is given something to eat, the demon "Legion" takes possession of a whole herd of swine, the lepers are certified by the priests as healed. These stories do not, like the others, cause one to realize the nearness of the Kingdom of God but only the presence of a great miracle worker. Hence they report not only healings but also other miraculous deeds of Jesus, the so-called nature miracles.

Much that we seize upon in these "novelistic" Tales as distinctive in contrast to the more concise stories, the "Paradigms," may be due simply to the difference in style: an event was reported in the manner of popular miracle narration, with the inevitable result that there took place a height-

ening of the miraculous. In such a case we can only guess at
the original event. But there is no question that a historical
occurrence of some kind, a cure or a rescue from danger at
sea, did really take place.

In other cases, the emphasis of the narrative falls upon an
event that had symbolical meaning for the Christian community. In such stories the community saw Jesus portrayed in
a function that belonged to him as Lord or Son of God. The
actor in this given instance was the exalted Lord, not the
Master who journeyed about Galilee. They beheld him in his
epiphany (i.e., in his divine rank), already exalted a stage
above all historical events. The historical occasion had perhaps existed, but we can no longer reconstruct it, because the
narrator himself lays the decisive emphasis on something
else. An epiphany of this sort is given, e.g., in the story of
the transfiguration (Mark 9:2–9), according to which Jesus
is snatched up from a mountaintop into the heavenly sphere,
between Moses and Elijah. In this instance Jesus himself does
nothing miraculous, but the miracle is worked on him from
heaven, and a heavenly voice proclaims him as God's Son.
But perhaps also the walking on the water was originally
an epiphany, for Jesus does not actually appear to the disciples on the water in order to proceed with them to land,
but — as is still clearly to be read in Mark (ch. 6:48) — " he
meant to pass by them." It is their fright that first moves
him to get into the boat with them. The community was
thus to see in this story the Lord of the waves; perhaps it
signified at the same time that he is the Lord over life and
death. In any case the walking on the water is not meant as
the special accomplishment of a saint or pious man. It is in
this latter sense that the Buddhist tradition tells of a devout
lay brother who, while engaged in contemplation upon
Buddha, walked across a river. Only when he had reached

the middle of the river was he diverted by the sight of the waves from his meditation on Buddha and his feet began to sink; but by renewed concentration of his thoughts on Buddha he became master of his insecurity and happily arrived at the opposite bank. This is a parallel to the story of the sinking Peter (Matt. 14:28–31), who comes to grief through lack of faith as did the Indian through the diverting of his thoughts; but the Indian tale is essentially different from the story of Jesus' appearance on the waves.

So too the story of the feeding of the five thousand or of the four thousand (Mark 6:34–44; 8:1–9) was understood in the community as an " epiphany," indeed was perhaps told as such from the outset. One sees in the Master who blesses and distributes the food the Lord of the Love Feast or Agapê (or even of the Last Supper) who is invisibly present to his community as he was visibly present to that great throng. Finally, the three raisings of the dead which are narrated in the Gospels and report the miraculous return to life of Jairus' daughter, of the young man of Nain, and of Lazarus, aimed at portraying the Lord of life and death, who, according to John 11:25, is " the resurrection and the life." Jesus is the vanquisher of death, but, according to primitive Christian belief, he first became this through his own resurrection. So in reality these miracle stories are already depicting the exalted Lord of the community.

Of course one may ask, in the case of these last examples, the stories of miraculous feedings and of the raising of the dead, whether foreign, i.e., extra-Christian, traits have not been woven into the portrayal. That is, to be sure, a possibility with which one has to reckon, and this recognition prevents us from being entirely certain whether or not a historical occasion for these stories was present in the life of Jesus. It is probable that now and then the Christians appropriated to themselves and transferred to their Saviour not only foreign motives but also whole stories of foreign origin. There are at bottom, however, only three instances where whole stories suggest such an origin. One tells of the demon Legion who, on going out of the sick man, drives a whole herd of swine into the water (Mark 5:1–17). All misgiving about the damage done the owners would disappear if we could assume that this entire incident was not originally one told about Jesus, but about a Jewish miracle man who undertook this expulsion in some heathen country, and hence felt no sympathetic concern either for the men or for the unclean animals. Likewise, the story of the wedding feast at Cana, though it is certainly understood in the Gospel of John as the revelation of Jesus' glory (ch. 2:11), betrays in its actual course certain secular features which any Bible reader can detect. One thinks, e.g., of the great amount of water turned into wine, and of the charming way in which the finished miracle is reported indirectly — in the bluff and hearty reproach of the bridegroom by the steward. Here, as in the case of the (not reported but only promised) finding of a coin in the mouth of a fish (Matt. 17:27), one can recall extra-Christian parallels which at least show that the substance of the story was known elsewhere too.

The result of our survey of the great miracle stories, reported in the form of Tales, is therefore this: that they elude a single uniform estimate. We may have to do with a further development of old traditions, with Christian portrayals of the exalted Lord, or with foreign motives or materials that have been transferred to Jesus; what lies behind these Tales in the way of historical reality is hardly accessible to us. But we know from the simpler healing stories that those great miracles were attributed to Jesus because he really had done things that were extraordinary and inexplicable to the minds of his contemporaries. He proceeded through the country as a herald, a judge, and a counselor, but also as a healer and a helper; from this historical statement of fact there is nothing to be stricken out.

But of course the healings are not to be isolated. Jesus did not come forth as a miraculous physician whose mission it was to make as many sick folk as possible well. Whoever makes him the patron of a method of religious healing, e.g., of Christian Science, has misunderstood him. If he had wanted to be anything of that sort he would have healed more persons, he would have extended his healing activity systematically over the country, he would also have said more about it. Suffering, including physical suffering, is a characteristic mark of this world; only God's Kingdom will show once more the finished creation, untouched by pain. Jesus' cures do not signify an arbitrary anticipation of this Kingdom, which no man knows when God will send. On the contrary, they signify the proclamation and promise of this Kingdom; they prove that it is on the way, that God, through the One whom he has sent, is already permitting the splendor of this Kingdom to shine out here and there.

Here and there — this also holds good for everything Jesus communicates to the world in the way of warning or instruction. Accordingly, his words do not set forth a basic program for the reform of this world. And if a section of the Sermon on the Mount gives the impression that Jesus was systematically revising the application of the Ten Commandments, it is these very sayings that show how many questions remain unanswered, indeed are not even considered. Jesus did not set out to settle all the affairs of this world, nor to remove all examples of social injustice. He opposed them only where he came upon them; he also caused the powers of the coming Kingdom to shine here, but he did not anticipate this Kingdom. Whoever makes him out to be a world reformer has also misconstrued him.

But, to be sure, he *did* act; he intervened in the sphere of illness and in that of injustice, and he set himself against the course of this world. He did not merely talk about the coming Kingdom of God, but he brought home to men its promises and also its demands — through what he did, through his judging, warning, healing. But he did it by way of example, as occasion offered, not systematically, not by organizing it on a large scale. The transformation of the world is God's affair; what Jesus does is to make men recognize this God, his will, his judgment, and his grace, in every event of life. The powers of the Kingdom are already present, yet not as a force that changes the world but as the strength that radiates from One, the only one, who is familiar with it and mediates it. What he makes men see in the form of healing or of encouragement, of criticism and of promise, is not the Kingdom but the *signs* of this Kingdom. To that extent certainly, but only to that extent, "the Kingdom of God is in your midst." And the One who brings all this in the last hour, who not only announces it but through his own activity mediates it, is himself the sign that it *is* the last hour, the only sign of the Kingdom of God that is vouchsafed to men.

Thus Jesus' message and Jesus' deeds cannot be separated from his person. And so the question arises how he himself wanted to be regarded.

VII

THE SON OF MAN

What significance did Jesus ascribe to himself? Did he regard himself as the Messiah, the Anointed of God, to whom the hopes of his people pointed, as the one who should renew the glorious kingdom of David and restore their freedom to the people of Israel, now ruled over by the Romans? Did he believe that he was chosen by God to appear to the world on the clouds of heaven "like a Son of Man," as the Redeemer of the world predicted in apocalyptic books? In the learned as well as in the popular religious literature of the preceding century, this question has been raised again and again — and with widely differing results. It seems strange that after such long efforts no clear answer should be found. It seems still more strange that the Gospels should not contain consistent evidence on the subject, which would silence all doubt.

Our first task is to understand why doubt is possible, why caution is demanded, and why critical reflection is justified. Our Gospels are — as we have observed all along — books that set out to establish faith in Jesus as the Christ, the Messiah. Thus we read at the end of the Gospel of John (ch. 20:31): "But these signs are written in order that you may believe that Jesus is the Christ, the Son of God, and that from such faith you may have life in his name." What is here expressly set as subscript under one Gospel stands unwritten under all: Jesus is the Christ.

But what did the Evangelists, what did the growing Church, understand by " Christ," the " Messiah," or — as our translation for both titles runs — the " Anointed " of God ? Here lies the first difficulty. The Evangelists look back. They know Jesus not only as put to death but as risen and exalted to God's side " from whence he shall come again to judge the living and the dead." They speak out of the Easter faith, and for this faith the word " Messiah," i.e., " Christ," has a new meaning: it designates the rank that belongs to Jesus and to no one else. Before the resurrection, the word had not been determined by the events but by the expectation; everybody could import into it what he hoped for. To many, the life and work of Jesus seemed better fitted to awaken doubt as to his Messiahship than faith. Had it been otherwise, John the Baptist would not have sent his messengers to Jesus. The Evangelists, wherever they touch the question of Messiahship, already speak of the Messiah in the Christian sense, so that all doubt as to Jesus' Messiahship is excluded. In all passages that come under consideration, words and deeds that relate to the Messiah are thus given a Christian interpretation, so that the Passion and resurrection, for example, already belong to it. The Gospels depict what the community believed about Jesus, not what he himself and what others thought about him in his lifetime. Therefore all these passages, strictly taken, are not sources for the pre-Easter, but for the post-Easter, the Christian, period.

Even our oldest Gospel, that according to *Mark,* must be understood thus. The picture that Mark draws is this: in spite of his words and deeds Jesus was not recognized by the people as Messiah. That he is the Messiah, only the super-terrestrial and subterrestrial beings know, not men. For that reason, only the persons who are " possessed " by demons, i.e., the demons themselves, address Jesus as the Messiah; but Jesus forbids them to spread this knowledge farther: he wants to be sure that his Messiahship is kept a secret (see, e.g., Mark 3:11, 12). In the same way Jesus forbids the publication of his great miracle acts, the raising of the girl, the healing of the deaf-and-dumb man and of the blind man of Bethsaida. And when Peter in answer to Jesus' question utters the great saying, "You are the Messiah," Jesus answers here again with the command not to spread this recognition farther (ch. 8:29, 30). Once only, the most intimate disciples behold him for an instant in a transfigured, heavenly state; but they are immediately forbidden to tell anyone of it "until the Son of Man is risen," i.e., until he has returned forever to that transfigured heavenly state (ch. 9:9). Thus in Mark's Gospel heavenly vision and human uncertainty are bound together: Jesus was the Messiah and could not deny this even during his earthly life; but he wanted his status kept secret, for—this is manifestly the leading thought in Mark—only thus is to be explained the fact that these men, his contemporaries and fellow countrymen, finally delivered him to the Romans to be crucified.

A quite different picture is drawn by *Matthew,* at least of that scene in which Peter recognizes and confesses the Messiah. Jesus' answer is a beatitude upon the disciple to whom God has granted this recognition. Then Jesus continues: "And I say to you, that you are Peter [the rock], and on this rock I will build my Church, and the gates of Hades shall not prevail against it. I will give to you the keys of the Kingdom of Heaven; what you bind on earth shall be bound in heaven; what you shall loose on earth shall be loosed in heaven" (Matt. 16:18, 19). And then only after the above follows the command of silence, as in Mark.

It is a sort of founding of the Church—and one may well

ask whether at this moment Jesus already looked forward to a Church. Furthermore, one may ask why Mark did not include these words, if they had already been transmitted in this connection in his day. Obviously they had not been, at least not in connection with this incident, for Luke too is ignorant of them. They speak of the founding of the Church and of the right to bind and loose within the Church, i.e., to pronounce guilty or not guilty. They reflect in the form of a prophetic promise a situation that the Evangelists know from experience: the Church is founded to endure permanently, and it possesses the right to forgive sins or to retain them. It is a sublime picture that Matthew gives us. But it is a Christian, a post-Easter, picture!

Thus the recognition that all the passages that speak of Jesus' Messiahship have been done over from the Christian point of view gives rise to the question whether or not Jesus knew himself to be the Messiah. The question is justified. The classic passage, Peter's confession of the Messiah, does not give an unambiguous answer to the question, since the oldest tradition does not tell us how Jesus received that confession of the disciple. But perhaps we can get closer to the problem if we consider the traditions having to do with Jesus' stay in Jerusalem.

In the first place, Jesus' journey to Jerusalem at the time of the Passover is itself loaded with meaning. For Jesus does not, like others, enter the capital city as a festival pilgrim. He seeks there, as we have already seen (p. 62), nothing less than the final decision. The call to make ready for the Kingdom of God is carried from the province to the capital — that signifies a deliberate challenging of the leading circles of the Jewish religion, those who regard themselves as God's professional counselors, the scribes, and the members of the Sanhedrin or " Chief Council." John gave expression to their thought when he had them say to Nicodemus (ch. 7:52), "Search, and see that no prophet arises out of Galilee." In this instance the prophet does come out of Galilee, and the multitudes — especially, perhaps, the Galilean pilgrims, but also certain circles from the capital — prepare for him a triumphal reception.

Of course here too the tradition is borne along by Christian interests. Jesus enters Jerusalem riding on an ass. This signifies a fulfillment of the Prophet Zechariah's prediction of the king, "meek and riding on an ass," who would come to the "daughter of Zion." According to the three oldest Gospels, Jesus acquired his mount by means of miraculous knowledge; according to John's Gospel it was only later on, "when Jesus was glorified," that the disciples became aware that with this entry they had unwittingly fulfilled the prophecy. So here again the account is shaped by a miracle; the fulfillment of the prophetic words is the main thing, not the historical context, i.e., the enthusiasm of the multitude, and the expectations, perhaps of a political sort, to which it gave rise. Yet it does not necessarily follow from this that the entry into Jerusalem is unhistorical.

The entry signifies at any rate an event fraught with Messianic significance. And associated with it, according to the Synoptic narrative, on the same day or soon after, is the ejection of the traders from the forecourt of the Temple, the so-called cleansing of the Temple. Now this is really a public appearance of Jesus at the center of the Jewish cultus, the strongest kind of challenge to all those who were hitherto in control there. But of course it is not absolutely a Messianic act, one of those that were expected from the Anointed of God. Even a prophet, acting in God's name and in a representative capacity, could exercise the right of sovereignty in the Temple. Yet nothing is said in the story about any representative capacity. Even so, the final impression remains that Jesus acted in this instance as Lord, as Son, as Messiah. One has also every right to ask how such a proceeding was possible for an unknown Galilean. Why did not the authorities interfere, either the Jewish or the Roman? Had so many of his adherents crowded into the Temple with him that they held possession of the place, if only for a day? On these points we have no information, and therefore it is plausible to see in the event only the expression of a moral authority. This was undoubtedly present, otherwise the Jews would not have given Jesus free scope. One is reminded of the boy Jesus, how, according to the story in Luke 2:46, asking and answering questions in the Temple at the age of twelve, he threw the teachers of his people into astonishment, and not less so his parents: " Did you not know that I must be in my Father's house? " In a similar way he may now as a man have claimed a sovereign right in the holy house. We are thus brought very near, at this point, to accepting a Messianic estimate of his person.

A decision of the Messianic question may more readily be reached from the account of Jesus' crucifixion. We know nothing for certain regarding the conduct of his trial, for the Evangelists had no one to rely on who had been an eyewitness of the proceedings. Therefore Jesus' confession before the high priest cannot be included without question in this chain of evidence, for the witnesses of the scene were restricted in number and of a kind not accessible to the Christians. But doubtless the crucifixion of Jesus, like all executions at that time, took place with the fullest publicity, and everybody knew what the crime was that was to be atoned for by such an execution; either a herald announced the guilt of the offender or it was set forth on a placard. Eyewitnesses of the crucifixion were known to the earliest com-

munity (Mark 15:21); for this reason we can trust the report that Jesus' offense was publicly posted (ch. 15:26). All
four Evangelists know that Jesus was designated on this
placard as "king of the Jews." This is the form, then, in
which the title of Messiah had been made intelligible to the
Roman procurator. Jesus was crucified because he was ac-
cused of laying claim to the throne, of aspiring to be Messiah. There must, accordingly, have been something in his
way of speaking and acting that gave this charge a certain
amount of justification.

He must have set forth the claim, although in a different
sense from what the Roman thought and from what the
Jew made the Roman believe, to be the Anointed of God.
But this is antecedently probable, anyway. It was a time of
political tensions and of revolutionary agitations. Again and
again, people had been coming forward with promises of a
Messianic kind. Anyone who proclaimed, as Jesus did, the
imminent arrival of the Kingdom of God, or revealed the
forces of this Kingdom already active in the present, or led
his followers to Jerusalem, as the scene of decisive action —
such a leader had to face the question whether he himself
was going to be the Promised One. In his case, the question
had only to do with the future; Kingdom, like Messiahship,
comes from God. One cannot, even Jesus cannot, *be* Messiah
by virtue of his own right; one can only, and Jesus can only,
trust, believe, know that God has chosen him to be Messiah
and will install him as Messiah in his Kingdom. Within the
time frame of this world the Messiah is only designated, not
enthroned.

Jesus knew himself to be the Messiah chosen by God, especially when he made his entrance into Jerusalem and appeared in the Temple as Lord. And now as one casts one's
eye backward the evidential force of the other testimonies

becomes stronger, not of the individual events but in their interconnection and sequence. It now seems no longer incredible that a disciple, interrogated by Jesus himself, should have spoken forth his faith in Jesus' future Messianic dignity. Everything that Jesus did and said has its own special importance — if it is not merely the announcement of what another is going to do but is the anticipatory realization of the events to which the speaker himself is called. When two disciples of Jesus plead for the places of honor at his side, in his Kingdom, they must be speaking with the conviction that he is going to be the king of the coming Kingdom (Mark 10:37). When a woman anoints the head of the Master as he reclines at the table, she is honoring him in the way one honors a king; she sees in him the king of God's Kingdom (ch. 14:3–7). The shouting throng at the entry — and even his enemies at the Temple cleansing who, however, make no attempt to interfere — either recognize or at least suspect in Jesus' person the Messiah-to-be.

Of course, in spite of all this, it is still not decided with what title the coming king was honored. Obviously the word "Messiah" did not have the wide circulation or the significance that we more or less unconsciously assume. In the Synoptic tradition the expression "Son of Man" is much more frequent; in the three oldest Gospels it occurs — leaving out the infancy and Passion narratives — more than three times as often as the title "Messiah." This is to be explained on the ground of the special ideas and expectations that, for the Christians, were bound up with the phrase "Son of Man." Apocalyptic writings like the Book of Enoch designated by this name the world Redeemer who was to come from heaven and who at the same time bore the out-

ward semblance of a man (see p. 47). The name may have
been connected originally with the ancient Persian doctrine,
according to which the "primal man," the first to be created, would appear again at the end of the ages. There
were other conceptions, according to which this primal man
did not live and die as a man but, as a semidivine being,
existed with God in heavenly concealment only to be revealed at the end of the whole series of world ages. The
Apostle Paul refers to this doctrine when he distinguishes
the "earthly" Adam from the "spiritual" Adam (i.e.,
"man"!) and adds, "Now it is not the case that the spiritual
appears first, but rather the earthly, and only after that the
spiritual" (I Cor. 15:46). Here, of course, the assumption is
that the Son of Man is the coming Messiah or, as the Book
of Enoch says, the "Elect One," i.e., the Chosen of God.
However, the idea of the concealment of the Son of Man
provided the first Christians with the key that unlocked for
them the earthly life of Jesus. For, finally, the earthly life of
Jesus and its ignominious end, and all that was repugnant
and humiliating in the historical existence of Jesus, still belonged to this concealment. And "must not the Messiah
suffer these things, in order to enter into his glory" (Luke
24:26)? Yes, and "heaven must receive him until the time
when all things return to a fresh beginning" (Acts 3:21).
Thus the belief in the Son of Man afforded the guarantee
that the work of redemption was not yet fully carried out
and that Jesus would come again in glory as the manifest
Son of Man, and thus enter definitively into his Messiahship.
Thus the Son of Man doctrine helped the first communities
to overcome the difficult riddle of the cross. They envisaged
the coming Messiah in the figure of the Son of Man — this
is the Christian way of understanding the Son of Man
doctrine.

But it still remains to be asked whether Jesus himself did not already move in a similar circle of ideas. He could speak of the coming Son of Man, without referring to himself (e.g., Luke 17:24; Mark 8:38). In Jesus' Aramaic speech the expression "son (or child) of man" was not distinguished from "man"; yet he spoke mysteriously, though clearly enough for everyone who shared these expectations of the day or the coming of "the Man." There are also, however, among the transmitted words of Jesus, some in which the most paradoxical statements are made regarding the Son of Man: that he goes hence, and that he will be delivered into the hands of sinners. Often enough, it is true, these sayings already reflect the Christian interpretation of Jesus' career, and the Evangelist is in such cases more interpreter than narrator. But at least one saying does have reference to the presence of the historical man Jesus; he answers one who would go with him as a disciple:

"The foxes have holes,
And the birds of heaven have nests,
But the Son of Man does not know where he can lay his head"
(Matt. 8:20).

Thus it was possible for Jesus to speak in such a way as to suggest the contrast between the obscurity of his indigent earthly existence and the glory of the "Man" from heaven —the contrast and at the same time the connection—for the needy life belongs to the concealment of the Son of Man and points to the future.

The preference for the expression "Son of Man" in the Christian tradition shows in any case that the Christians knew of no *political* activity on the part of their Master. "Son of David" and "Messiah" would permit a political interpretation; "Son of Man" means the one sent into the world by God, not the heir of David's throne and the emancipator from the Roman rule. Anyone who sets out to maintain that Jesus planned an attack on the Roman forces of occupation or on the Jewish authorities is compelled to deny the whole tradition: not only the sayings about turning the other cheek or about service, but also the promises of the Kingdom which God will bestow upon the humble-minded, those who are detached from the world and, although in the world, are cut off from it. If Jesus had meant to gain political leadership, he would have had to choose his adherents differently; he would have had to give more thought to winning the masses and to gaining public success; he would have had to carry on his mission in the prominent cities of the country (see p. 62); and he would have had in word and deed to rouse his disciples to action and inspire them with zeal to battle against the existing order. He did just the opposite of all this. And if it so happens that he himself did drop the Messianic title, but employed the expression " Son of Man " — both with and without reference to himself — that is a confirmation of his nonpolitical attitude. The sword which he says that he brings (Matt. 10:34) goes, as the rest of the saying shows, through families and not through nations.

There are two situations within the Synoptic tradition that permit the reader to peer deeply into Jesus' attitude toward the hope of his nation, and also explain why Jesus did not say yes without more ado to all Messianic glorification, and yet did not reject his nation's hope. The first of these situations is the scene where Jesus sends his answer to the Baptist (see pp. 76 ff.). John asks: " Are you the Messiah? " and Jesus answers, in substance, " The Kingdom of God is coming; and blessed is he who takes no offense at me." The question of personal estimate falls into the background; it is the

Kingdom toward which faith ought to be directed. The
second scene is not quite so well attested historically, for it
can hardly rest on the report of reliable witnesses, and yet
it lays claim to the truth of the inner situation. It is the examination before the high priest. He asks, "Are you the
Messiah, the Son of the Blessed?" And Jesus answers with
a clear affirmation, "I am, and you shall see the Son of Man
sitting at the right hand of Majesty and coming with the
clouds of heaven." Thus the hope of the nation confronts
Jesus once more, with a tone of interrogation, in his last
hour. He does not, however, speak of the throne of David
but of the throne of God. It is in that direction, and toward
the coming in splendor of the Son of Man, that the eyes of
the judges ought to be turned; for the redemption of the
world is something more than any Messianic activity (Mark
14:61 f.).

Speaking in general, we may say that the events of the
Passion story, above all, the Last Supper, can be far better
understood if Jesus intended to leave behind him on earth
a circle instructed by him, one devoted to the Messianic expectation, as a witness and pledge of a personal attachment
to him. And there are also certain sayings in which Jesus
speaks of himself and of his purpose that permit us to sur-
mise that he intended himself to be the leader and the inaug-
urator of God's Kingdom: so with the twin sayings about
the fire that he is to kindle and the baptism that he is to un-
dergo (Luke 12:49 f.).

We might go still farther. We might conjecture that for
Jesus the one is not possible apart from the other, the Messianic rank not apart from the thought of suffering. We
might assume that the more probable the prospect of suffering and death became to Jesus the more certainly he antici-

pated his installation as Messiah. But all such suppositions go beyond what the accounts of the Gospels say or suggest. They do not set out to give a portrayal of Jesus' inner life, nor to tell about inner changes or developments. The aim of their narration is rather to enable their readers to recognize Jesus' true rank even during his earthly life. Hence one may draw from the tradition only that particular answer to the Messianic question which may be gathered from the tradition as a whole, without reinterpreting it or reading into it something that is not really there.

Let us now attempt to survey the various considerations that have been set forth in this chapter and to sum up the final impression. This above all is clear, clear beyond all doubt, that during his ministry Jesus did not set the question of Messiahship in the foreground. The designation of his person with the appropriate title (Messiah, Son of Man, Son of David, etc.) is not a condition of salvation. One is to see in his acts God's working, one is to perceive in his appearing God's coming with his Kingdom — that is what Jesus demands, but not the confession of his Messiahship.

But it is also clear that Jesus intends to do more than merely announce the Kingdom of God. The fact that he can speak with full authority as he does, that he can ask men to recognize the forces of God's Kingdom in his healings, even now before this Kingdom has appeared — that is in itself a proof of the fact that God's Kingdom is drawing near. Jesus himself, in his own person, in his words and deeds, is the decisive sign of the Kingdom. Therefore he insists that men must recognize the signs of the times; that is why in all his promises and commands he can appear before men with a

claim that is more than human, that he can ride into Jerusalem as king of peace, and take charge in the Temple as
Lord.

The term "Messiah" is susceptible of many interpretations and not every one of them would come up to Jesus'
conception. Perhaps for this reason Jesus spoke more often
of the Son of Man than of the Messiah. The term "Son of
Man" includes the thought that the Man from heaven who
will appear at the end of the world is first to be hidden for
a time. Such a concealment — in spite of all the signs that he
performed — was Jesus' earthly life and suffering.

That in this sense Jesus affirmed his rank as Son of Man or
Messiah is also shown, finally, by his execution as pretender
to the throne. It is the proof of the fact that he actually did,
during his lifetime, make the claim that he would sometime
become Ruler, Messiah, or Redeemer. So then his words, sayings, groups of sayings, and parables must not be viewed as
the occasional utterances of a rabbi. They are to be understood as the proclamation of a lofty commission, as commands of God spoken through a human voice. Only then
do these words bear their proper, deeply serious import.

VIII

MAN'S STATUS BEFORE GOD

Threat, promise, demand — this the frame within which Jesus' teaching about the Kingdom of God is confined. That God will shortly enter into the world must seem like a *threat* to an indifferent human race, immersed in the life of instinct, or to an ambitious one, entangled in prejudices. It sees itself suddenly challenged by One who passed through this world as a witness for the world of God and a living sign of its coming. The transformation of things which he announced seemed in itself to be something threatening; hard times would precede it. What was required was utter loyalty, the refusal to fear those who might kill the body: " Let your loins be girded and your torches burning! "

To all those, however, who doubted or despaired over the meaning of life, to whom it had become a question in their own lives why this world, created by God, served God's purposes so slightly — to them Jesus brought the message of the Kingdom of God as *promise*. A time would come, and it was already very close, when God himself in the person of his Anointed would take control of this world. Then the contradictions within the world order would begin to make sense; injustice, the fact that might takes precedence of right among the nations as well as in the existence of a single people, would disappear; then it would become evident who is the Lord of the world — in the Kingdom of God. That is why

Jesus clothes the promise in a call to the disinherited and oppressed of this world:

" Blessed, you poor — yours is the Kingdom of God!
   Blessed, you that hunger — you shall be satisfied!
   Blessed, you that weep — you shall laugh!
   Blessed are you, when they revile you and speak evil of you!
   Rejoice and be glad! A great reward is awaiting you in heaven! "
                              (Luke   :20, 21; Matt. 5:11, 12).

Thus he foresees a complete reversal of the claim to the
Kingdom. From afar, out of the East and the West, they will
come and find entrance. Those, however, who call themselves " sons of the Kingdom " will be cast out into everlast-
ing darkness — " misery is there, and shuddering, and tor-
ment " (Matt. 8:11, 12).

It is no wonder that the men thus set between threat and
promise are eager to know how they can escape the threat
and become partakers of the promise. They want to hear
God's *requirement* from the herald and witness of the Kingdom. As a matter of fact, Jesus did give counsel in the name
of God, in great fundamental questions as well as in minor
matters. But Jesus was no lawgiver. If he had been, his detailed instructions would have had to embrace the whole
area of human life. Instead, his admonitions by no means
deal with all the questions that life presents, and many of
the problems of human life are simply not considered (cf.
p. 87). Only by way of example does he take up such questions or let them be submitted to him: the customs of his people, even the religious customs such as fasting and prayer,
furnish the occasion for such questions. The Gospels have
preserved to us a comparatively large number of such instructions — some with and some without the occasion being given. That explains the misconception, appearing ever
and again in new forms, that the Gospel is a collection of

commandments, that discipleship means the carrying out of a number of precepts.

This is probably the most serious misconception that encumbers the tradition of Jesus, and especially, as part of this tradition, that most systematic arrangement of Jesus' teaching in the Gospels, the Sermon on the Mount (Matt., chs. 5 to 7). This Sermon is a collection of Jesus' words, short sayings and connected groups of sayings, whose genesis one can discover for himself in the briefer parallels to be found in Luke 6:20–49. There was obviously already to be found among the sources of the two Gospels, Luke and Matthew, a short presentation of Jesus' teaching, which consisted of the fragments that both Evangelists record at the same point. This must have begun with the Beatitudes and closed with the parable of the Two Houses; in between, it contained sayings that called for the renunciation of retaliation and for the love of enemies, after which followed the sayings about judging, about the tree and its fruits, and about " Lord, Lord." Even this first little collection, found in the lost source, undertook not only to give an impressive example of the teaching of Jesus, but at the same time to sketch out what it meant to be a Christian in the midst of the world. How much the more was this the aim of Luke, and — especially — of Matthew! In the case of Matthew, it is not only in the selection and arrangement but also in the wording of the sayings that one can recognize a concern to set forth the requirements for the Christian life. Jesus' call to the disinherited and downtrodden among his hearers, " Blessed, you poor," has become the statement (in the third person instead of the second), " Blessed are those who are poor in spirit " — a restricted statement, for the addition of the words " in spirit " is meant to prevent misunderstanding, e.g., that Jesus had pronounced the blessing upon poverty as such. The addition is intended to restrict the Beatitude to the group of those who are inwardly oppressed by the course of things, and thus it runs counter to the original meaning of the words as given by Luke. In Matthew, attached to these Beatitudes on the disinherited and oppressed, are other sayings of Jesus which similarly exalt the meek, the merciful, the sincere (" the pure in heart "), and the peacemakers. Thus the call to the poor and hungry becomes a catalogue of Christian virtues. And, in like manner, all the sayings of the Sermon on the Mount appear to have been put together to form a kind of catechism dealing with the life of the Christian in the world.

This, however, is the result of a transformation that had already taken place. The Christian communities, confronted with the demands and cares of daily life, craved an answer to the question, How are we to live as Christians in the midst of the world? The hearers of Jesus, on the other hand, had asked, What kind of people are we to be when the new world breaks in?

Therefore it is not correct to separate these sayings of the Sermon on the Mount from other words of Jesus — words of warning and of promise, but words which in every case point to the Kingdom of God — and to describe them as "basic principles" of Jesus' preaching, i.e., as commandments that do not assume the approaching transformation of the world, but set out to regulate the life of the Christians in the world as it now is. Originally these "basic" sayings likewise had reference to the coming of the Kingdom. How could it have been otherwise in a preaching that sought to prepare men for the Kingdom! How could one expect anything else from a proclaimer who stands before his hearers as a visible sign of the coming Reign of God! All his commandments and requirements are part of his message of the Kingdom of God, rather than appropriate measures for the reform of this present world; in all of them, in the most intelligible as in the strangest of them, the coming of the Kingdom is either tacitly or explicitly taken for granted as the major presupposition. The command is given, not in order that thereby the Kingdom may come, but because it is coming. It is a question of laying hold on men with God's command and preparing them for the Kingdom's coming. While in the command Jesus proclaims God's will in the presence of God's Kingdom, he himself appears — and doubtless appeared to many among his hearers — not only as the announcer but also as the fulfiller of that will. He speaks " as one who possesses authority and power " (Matt. 7:29), and this authority does not first need to be validated by means of his office or his Scriptural theology. Similarly a consideration of his demands awakens an understanding of his rank (see Chapter VII).

Jesus' words, like his deeds, are signs of the coming Kingdom. He gives no new law that embraces all the circumstances of life. Precisely the fact that the tradition of his words is silent regarding many problems of life is proof to us of this sign quality. He speaks to his own people, and in so doing remains within the frame of the traditional religion. If the nation had really heard Moses and the prophets, it would doubtless have been ready for the Kingdom. But precisely the ordinances of the old Jewish religion became for him, ever and again, the occasion for the revealing of signs of the new thing, the new behavior of men in the presence of the coming God. He sees the devout of his nation fasting: they creep around with woe-begone countenances in order to show to everybody how pious they are (for fasting is a pious but, of course, voluntary practice). Are such people ready for the Kingdom? No, says Jesus. Let them wash and anoint themselves as if they were

going to a banquet. That would be real fasting in the sight of
God (Matt. 6:16–18)! This is said in that Oriental fashion
which does not set out to describe something, but rather to
rouse the will by overstatement and exaggeration. It is not
dissimulation that Jesus preaches, but reserve; not a new kind
of hypocrisy in place of the old, but an honesty in God's sight
that renounces all esteem in the eyes of men; for to accept the
praise of men means cheating God, to whom alone belongs
praise.

But Jesus, who speaks in this way about the right sort of
fasting, was once asked why his own disciples did not fast. In
that instance he replied, " Can the wedding guests fast as long
as the bridegroom is with them? " If the Evangelist (Mark
2:20) then has Jesus point to the future, when the bridegroom
would be taken away from them, and when they would then
have a right to fast, this is understood as a justification for
fasting in the Church; and accordingly the addition doubtless
originated at a time when the Christians themselves prac-
ticed fasting. But in any case the difference is significant: an
injunction to the right kind of fasting in the Sermon on the
Mount, a dispensation from fasting here (and, if one will, a
reference to the introduction of fasting in the future). This
comparison does not reflect indecision, but, on the contrary, a
power of judgment regarding the pious tradition. It is not a
question of either doing away with fasting or of making it
generally binding; it is a question, whether one fasts or not,
of being rightly prepared for the Kingdom of God.

This is why the tax collector in the parable story (Luke
18:10–14) is held up as an example in contrast to the Pharisee;
the latter dares even in the sanctuary, in the very presence of
God, to speak boastfully of his own pious conduct. He does
not lie, he is " good " (according to the human use of the
word). but he makes it the basis of a claim. The tax collector,

on the other hand, is not really a " sinner " (according to the human use of the word), but he is conscious of the holiness of God and humbles himself before him. The constant danger under which every kind of piety in the world stands — that of becoming an end in itself and thereby a kind of heathenism — is classically depicted in this brief, imaginative, but perfectly human story of what took place one day in the Court of the Temple. And here too the exhortation finds its compelling motive, unspoken but insistent, in the coming of the Kingdom: How shall one who has fooled himself into thinking that he has done all that God requires stand in the judgment when the holy God himself appears before him?

This is indeed the first and the foremost demand of the message of Jesus: *Be ready for God's Kingdom.* Jesus himself lived in this state of readiness. But not as an activist, who day and night thinks of nothing else but the overturning of the old and the creating of the new. On the contrary, Jesus awaited everything from the Father: day and hour of the great transformation (Mark 13:32), share and honor in the Kingdom itself (Mark 10:40) — indeed, Jesus' reserve on the subject of the Messiahship (Chapter VII) no doubt reflects this same deep attitude of will, which claims nothing for itself, but accepts everything at the hand of God. At least it is certain that the command to go through suffering and death was likewise in a true sense " accepted " by him. If it had been otherwise, Jesus would have defended himself for the sake of God's cause, or in the interest of this cause would have fled, or might even have flung himself at death with the passion of a martyr. This final alternative, however, would have found expression in the scene of the arrest. We hear of nothing of the kind; what the Gospels describe is neither histrionic nor mutinous, but a simple, obedient march into the darkness. Even from his first public appearance Jesus' face is already turned toward the Kingdom of God, to the Kingdom alone, and to no worldly goal or ideal. Therefore all values, treasures, goals belonging to the realm of politics, of civilization, of human society, sink out of sight. But again one must guard against the wrong inference: they do not disappear because they are regarded as worthless or because ascetic zeal renounces them. They simply fade in the splendor which proceeds from the Kingdom of God — so completely is Jesus devoted to this one thing and prepared for this alone. It is a most audacious piece of human interference with this devotion of Jesus when his mother and brethren try to take him home (Mark 3:31). People think " he is out of his senses " (Mark 3:21); that attitude of being devoted only to the invisible that is to come is indeed something that oversteps the human norm. Jesus himself knows and recognizes and understands only what he pointed out to the bustling Martha: " You are anxious and troubled about many things, but only one thing is needful " (Luke 10:41, 42).

And he demands the same readiness now from his followers. It is not sentimentality and not subjective contemplativeness that Jesus wants, but obedience. For it is the great hour of God — they should observe the signs of the time (Luke 12:56) and obey God's call. It is a radical obedience that Jesus demands, one that knows nothing else than this one object. He portrays it in the picture of the man who buys the field in order to acquire the treasure buried in it, and in that of the merchant who seeks the costliest pearl: both give all that they have for this one thing (Matt. 13:44–46). Indeed, he does not shrink from taking a criminal as an example, perhaps one well known at the time, since the children of light can learn even from the children of darkness: that unjust steward who is put out of his office does not think of using excuses in order to hold onto his position; he thinks only how, with one final deceit, he can make his future secure while he still has the ability to do so (Luke 16:1-8).

To one who, in radical obedience, judges the whole world solely in the light of this one thing — God and his coming into the world — to him everything becomes worthless that can separate him from God. And it makes no difference in such a case whether it has the approval of men or not. Whether duty or burden — whatever it is that holds men back from being ready for the Kingdom — it has no longer any rights in this cosmic hour. Foremost among these fettering forces stand *possessions* and *sickness*. The way in which each of these was looked upon at the time demands special attention. We too know the stultifying power of wealth, and how concern over it can become an end in itself, with the millionaire as well as the smaller saver. But just as truly, and with a much wider range among men, beggarly poverty, the worry over a bare existence from day to day, seems to us to be a dismal burdening of life which can exclude altogether the thought of an otherworldly destiny and determination of life. It was different under the economic conditions of Jesus' time and country. Hospitality and all sorts of possibilities of sustenance prevented the housing question from ever growing serious (for it is lacking also in Jesus' sayings about worry); the problem of wearing apparel is not serious, and, in case of utter need, food can be gathered in the fields (Mark 2:23). The freedom of a poor, itinerant kind of life, moreover, such as Jesus led with his followers, entirely in the service of the one cause (see p. 59), may in fact bring men nearer to God rather than farther away from him. The property owner, on the other hand, who must always take care of what he has and be concerned for its increase, faces a far greater danger of leading a self-sufficient life. That continues until God intervenes, either with the coming of his Kingdom, or, as in Jesus' parable story in Luke 12:20, with sudden death. " What shall become then of all that you have gathered? "

Jesus' warning against anxiety extends to all whose concern over possessions, whether acquisition or increase, keeps them from recognizing God's claim upon their life. The warning is grounded in the seriousness of the last hour: " But strive after his Kingdom, and then you will receive the other things in addition " (Luke 12:31). But this reference to the seriousness of the hour only brings to radical expression what God is always and everywhere demanding from men in the way of decision. It is the decision between God and the world that the rich man avoids (see p. 59). Jesus did not preach against possessions; his wandering life was made possible, to some extent, by the help of those among his followers who were property owners. But he experienced the fact, only too often, that possessions come between a man and God; to these men of wealth his words apply: " Woe to you, for you have received your consolation " (Luke 6:24); and so does his hard saying, not to be softened by anything in the figure employed, " It is easier for a camel to go through a needle's eye than for a rich man to enter the Kingdom of God " (Mark 10:25). But this realization did not restrain him from trying to win over that same rich man; nor did it keep him back from the next rich man: " For with God all things are possible."

Jesus does not set out to " abolish " either wealth or suffering. But undoubtedly he means to show that God's call is meant for everyone, for the man who is entrenched behind his possessions as well as for the man who lies buried, as it were, under a mass of human prejudices. This holds good, above all, of the chronically *sick*. Jewish theology claims to explain all the fortunes of life, happiness as well as suffering, by reference to divine retribution. So for this theology there is no question but that the sick man must have committed an of-

fense against God; otherwise he just would not be sick. That
is why Jesus greets the man who seems hopelessly lame with
the words, " Your sins are forgiven " (Mark 2:5). For God's
dealing with men cannot be confined within the mathematics
of a pure doctrine of recompense. And just as in this one story
the healing appears as confirmation of the forgiveness of sins,
so in principle every healing performed by Jesus is intended
to proclaim that sickness is not banishment from God. Thus
every healing becomes a sign of the coming Kingdom, the indication of the true will of God. But the full realization of his
will takes place only in the Kingdom of God; those signs remain isolated, and sickness continues to exist during this
world age. Jesus did not abolish it, but only in occasional instances of sickness made clear God's will.

The Gospel preaches preparedness for God's Kingdom, but
there follows from this not only the setting aside of all hindrances; there is involved also the demand for positive renunciation. This we learn from the saying addressed to the rich
man; formulated more generally and more radically, it runs:

> " If your hand leads you into temptation, hack it off!
> Better for you to enter maimed into eternal life
> Than having both hands to go to hell! "
>
> (Mark 9:43).

Everyone sees that what is meant here is not mutilation but
renunciation, and that the cutting off of the hand — or of the
foot, or the plucking out of the eye — is only a symbol of the
resolute renunciation of everything that lessens the preparation for God. We ought also to recognize the figurative character of the saying about eunuchs (Matt. 19:12), which distinguishes, among various cases of castration, those who came
thus from their mother's womb, those who let themselves be
mutilated by men, and finally those who underwent castra-

tion for the sake of God's Kingdom. If the figure is really understood as a figure, then the saying does not speak of castration but of renunciation. Only, the renunciation of the first
class is not renunciation at all; that of the second has nothing
to do with God; and only in the case of the third is there a
genuine sacrifice which prepares the man for the Kingdom.
It is a sacrifice that is demanded; it is only through the narrow
gate that one enters into life, and the man who takes hold of
the plow and looks back is of no use.

The Gospel does not preach asceticism as an end in itself;
were that the case, then the second group in the eunuch saying
would have been commended. Moreover, the renunciation
would be limited to the field of lusts and sins, to what yields
pleasure and satisfies impulses. Jesus demands still more: he
demands, under certain circumstances, even the renunciation
of duties. Here one sees most clearly the difference from the
legal religion: the whole Jewish system of commandments
and prohibitions with its absolute jurisdiction comes in question, since God himself is entering into the world with absolute majesty, absolute justice and holiness. Even the Sabbath
commandment must be broken if God requires it, not human
frivolity. The family must not restrain one any longer, and
the dead father is not to be buried by the son (Matt. 8:22). To
be sure, where religious (i.e., cultic) duty and filial duty conflict with one another, filial duty of course takes precedence
(Mark 7:10-13). But every earthly duty is made relative by
the nearness of God's Kingdom. And all the more, such a
duty as that of paying poll tax to the foreign government of
occupation is not regarded as a duty at all in the moral sense,
but merely as the consequence of political fortune. The meaning of the oft-quoted, repeatedly misunderstood saying of
Jesus, " Render to Caesar what is Caesar's and to God what is
God's," is misconstrued if one takes the saying as the state-

ment of a principle bearing on the problem of "Church and State." The coin bears the emperor's image; therefore give it back to him! But you pious questioners should be thinking of higher duties: "Render to God what belongs to him!" (Mark 12:13–17).

Not the doing of a deed is the decisive thing, for that may differ in different cases, but the man who does it. He stands always before God, before the coming God! The message of the Kingdom makes him no better, morally, but it lays hold on his entire being and changes him. And what he says or does then is said or done with his eyes upon the Kingdom. "A tree is known by its fruit," a man by his bearing before God. This is why Jesus turns more than once to the "publicans and sinners," because they know their own lack before God and make no claims. Their sins are not really denied or regarded as negligible; but they need not form a barrier between man and God. God must be taken more seriously than all that.

This new existence before God — which is not a state of life but an ever-ready hearing and obeying — Jesus reiterated again and again in a series of commands. Because these commands set forth the pure will of God without compromise of any sort, they often seem impossible of fulfillment in this old world. But this realization does not free man from the duty to hearken to God. Moreover, it is not the case that these commands were intended to express merely an "interim ethic," that they were valid only for the time immediately preceding the end of this world. They cannot be completely fulfilled before the end, but only in the time following after, in the new world of the Kingdom of God. It was in this sense, e.g., that Jesus forbade oaths (Matt. 5:34). For God's absolute will forbids man to make God the guarantor of man's statements or intentions. To what extent the state or the courts in this present world are compelled to employ such assurances as oaths — this question is not even raised. It may be that Jesus himself would have bowed to such a necessity (Matt. 26:63, 64); in this untransformed world the pure will of God does not yet achieve its full realization.

As with the oath, so with divorce: " What God has joined together, let not man put asunder " (Mark 10:9)! The fact that there are marriages in this present world that are by no means true marriages in this sense does not enter into the discussion, since that has to do only with God's will and God's Kingdom. The consequences which men draw from the fact of such marriages, Jesus would judge in the same way that he judges all those ways of giving assurance by oath (Matt. 5:37); they only prove that all this sort of thing " belongs to the evil [of this present world]." In Matthew, to be sure, such consequences are already being considered; for in this Gospel, but only in it, there is inserted in the absolute prohibition of divorce the exception " save in a case of fornication " (Matt. 5:32; 19:9). But this very form of the saying shows that Jesus' words were already being used for the legal ordering of daily life, and that the proclamation of the coming Kingdom was being made over into a catechism for continued existence in the old world.

For Jesus himself, the commands that " were said to them of old time," i.e., in the Old Testament (and in the Jewish interpretation of the Law), furnish the frame into which he inserts the absolute demand of God. The Old Testament was able to point out God's will to men. But since men look at the letter instead of really listening to God, God's will has to be announced to them in its startling absoluteness, which often goes beyond human capacity for fulfillment in this present world. This is seen most clearly in the commandment forbidding murder. It is not the murderer alone who transgresses this commandment, but even the man who feels anger, and especially the man who gives offensive expression to it (Matt. 5:21, 22). In this way every old commandment was susceptible of being comprehended anew and at times even of being corrected. Again and again it will be seen that the radical new formulation goes beyond the limits of human ability within the relations of this present world. Again and again it must be emphasized, however, that this radical demand laid upon men is not to be reduced or watered down. It is precisely its radicalism that enables it to lay bare the actual situation of men and to make them receptive of the Gospel call to repentance. The deep truth of this " convicting " function of the Law was set forth more than once by Paul in his struggle for freedom from the Law (Rom. 3:20; 5:20; 7:9; Gal. 3:24). Jesus spoke of this too, but only in various hints which pointed to the reality of the pure will of God and the distance that separated men from the demands of the Law.

In some of these examples he only hinted at this new existence of men before God, and did not describe it. For in truth it never can be described, since man is being constantly placed in new life situations which are always demanding new decisions. Only in certain great key words can guiding hints be given; it is in this way that Jesus speaks of faith, prayer, and love.

Faith is the word that signifies the acceptance of this message of the Kingdom, the turning toward the emissary of God and to the divine salvation. Anyone who understands the signs of the Kingdom and who hears the call of God will also experience the forces of the Kingdom already at work: only faith experiences healings (Matt. 8:10), only the believer has a share in the forgiveness of sins (Mark 2:5). But it belongs to the very nature of faith that it turns to God with its sins and its need and accepts both forgiveness and help, without asking any question about its deserts or lack of them, without making comparisons or calculations. Jesus and his disciples lived in daily contact with a system of piety that was built on a rational computation of the relation of man to God, and thereby set itself up over God. For that reason, Jesus never tired of holding before his contemporaries and compatriots the fact that they must not prescribe to God how his grace and his wrath should be distributed. If we had been dealt with on the basis of justice only, we should have deserved no better fate than those who were crushed beneath the tower of Siloam, or the Galileans murdered by Pilate (Luke 13:1–5). And even if we succeed in doing everything that God has commanded, we indeed remain in the sight of God mere " unprofitable servants," " who have done nothing more than their duty " (ch. 17:7–10). In the last analysis, men stand before God not otherwise than the day laborers of the parable, with their utter lack of any legal claim (that was the rule in those days), men who must not make comparisons or find fault if others receive a better assignment of work and therefore a larger reward (Matt. 20:1–15). And if God has compassion precisely upon the seemingly lost, as a father has for his wayward child, so he who regards himself as " less " lost must not remonstrate with him (Luke 15:11–32). Therefore the right attitude before God and in view of the coming Kingdom is that of the child who still understands the art of receiving and having presents given him. For what Jesus means when he assigns the Kingdom to the childlike (Mark 10:14 f.) is not the innocence of the child — which one cannot grant — but that simplicity which surrenders itself without reservation and unquestioningly lets itself be given gifts. What is meant is the attitude we must take before God through faith.

And this is always lacking in us double-minded men, because we are constantly concerned about ourselves and entangled in the world's deceptions.

Anyone who accepts the message of salvation in faith accepts it as a child, and stands in a different relationship to God from that of men in the religions of the ancient world; he dares to be unconstrained, he has no need of any mediation nor any mediating persons; he is in immediate relation to God. That will and must show itself in his praying. In the unquestionable sayings of Jesus, *prayer* is not spoken of as it is in the Sermon on the Mount (Matt. 6:5), i.e., as a pious practice along with other pious practices. It is rather the chosen expression for the relation of men to God. It is not necessary for God to listen to the prayers of men, counted out one after the other. It is not necessary for the pious to render their prayers as a service to God. But it is doubtless necessary for the man who believes in the message of the Kingdom of God to turn himself with all his concern to God. It is doubtless no accident that Jesus makes clear this rule of prayer in a series of very human pictures. He shows the effect of petition in the case of average, yes, even of evil, men; and then the question is asked, Will not God hear, even more readily and attentively, when he is prayed to? The more crass the contrast between God and the human example, the more convincing the argument. There is the father who will certainly not offer a stone to his hungry son who asks for bread (Matt. 7:9). There is the ordinary man who gets out of bed to answer his neighbor's knocking, not out of friendship, but in order to be rid of his importunity (Luke 11:5–8). There is — worst example of all — the wicked judge who sees that the helpless, persecuted widow gets justice, in order that she may pester him no longer (Luke 18:2–7).

The really classical example of prayer, however, is the

Lord's Prayer; it is not a normal prayer, though often so used, but a charter of the new relation to God. It is neither ecstatic stammering, nor ritual litany, nor presumptuous demonstration. It belongs less in a history of prayer than in a history of faith. It does not so much answer to the requirement: Thus shalt thou pray, as it does the other: Thus shalt thou *be!*

We read the Lord's Prayer in the New Testament in two forms: Luke gives (ch. 11:2–4 in the oldest manuscripts) a shorter text than the usual one (Matt. 6:9–13), in which the so-called third and seventh petitions are entirely wanting, and the address is formed only by the word "Father." If this Lucan form should turn out to be the oldest, then the so-called first petition is doubtless to be included in the address: "Father, hallowed be thy name." And then the prayer would consist of three petitions: for the Kingdom, for daily bread, and for the forgiveness of sins past and for preservation from future ones ("forgive us our debts as we forgive our debtors, and lead us not into temptation"). This prayer in fact sums up everything that the Gospel proclaims: the coming of the Kingdom, and the removal of care and sin, the two great obstacles to a life of faith in the midst of this world. One who can really pray in this way has accomplished the turning to God and to his Kingdom that we call faith, and thereby also the turning to him who in the midst of the world is the living sign of the Kingdom of God. One who can pray in this way is concerned over radical obedience to the absolute will of God; but he knows also about the limitations set by this world, which again and again hinder the fulfilling of this will, and he strives daily, hourly, to be rid of these hindrances. In this prayer neither is faith in Jesus as the fulfiller expressly confessed nor is the obedience of the new man promised; one may say, as has often been said, that

every single one of these petitions could also be repeated by
a Jew. And yet only this faith and this obedience describe
the attitude before God in which alone the Lord's Prayer
can really be prayed in the sense of its author.

The third password of this attitude (besides faith and
prayer) is *love*. This word is to be understood only in the
context of the message of the coming Kingdom of God,
therefore only by starting from God's action, not from human judgments or feelings. It is not a matter of philan-
thropy, which seeks the divine spark in the most degraded
men, nor is it a matter of an all-embracing breadth of sym-
pathy, so that one cannot pass by any sighing creature without at least having his own tender heart soothed by the attempt to help. The source of the love that Jesus demands is
God's love, revealed in Jesus' message and Jesus' life, in so
far as both are signs of the divine Kingdom: God's love directed toward the unworthy — for all are unworthy, the
good and the bad. A symbol of this love is the sun, which
shines upon all; proofs of this love are forgiveness and healing, which are the portion of the childlike recipient, i.e., of
the believing man; the witness to this love, however, must
be the one who receives it. It will not do for the slave who
has been forgiven much to go out and force payment from
his fellow slave who owes him a small debt (Matt. 18:23-35).
It will not do for the man who has experienced God's love
to set up barriers now on his side, and bestow his love only
on a fellow member of his own race or class, or on some al-
leged " neighbor " and refuse it to another. Any man can be
my neighbor, if God sends him my way — that is the meaning of the classic example of unhesitating loving-kindness
set forth in the story of the Good Samaritan (Luke 10:30-37).

This unquestioning nature of love, which passes beyond all
human frontiers (still so unavoidable in this world), Jesus in-

sisted upon in the command to love one's enemies (Matt.
5:44). We have become accustomed to think in this connection of war and enmity between nations. And of course Jesus
did not exclude this thought. But national wars between independent countries did not fall within the circle of his experience; moreover, the most consuming hatred does not as
a rule prevail between hostile fronts, but between people
who are close to one another, dependent on one another, between neighbors, competitors, subordinates, and superiors.
This hatred, including what we call "righteous indigna-
tion," is what the command to love one's enemies is meant
to overcome. It does not demand some special achievement,
as though the disciple of Jesus was supposed to love just his
enemies and them only; but it indicates, after the manner
of such sharpened formulations, the border case before which
the love of man actually — and with justification, according
to human standards — stops short: surely one does not love
his enemies! One who has been touched by God's love for
sinners, who are God's "enemies," no longer recognizes such
limits. The command to answer the adversary not with resistance but with conciliation is similarly sharpened to a
point: "If anyone smites you on your right cheek, offer him
the other also" (Matt. 5:38–42). This situation, like the
others that are brought up elsewhere in the discourse, really
presents an extreme case. They are not meant symbolically,
of course, as only the radical expression of a mild sentiment;
nor are they meant legally, as though precisely this and only
this should be required, over and again. But of these demands the principle holds good: they are to be fulfilled lit-
erally, where fulfillment is possible, not in a silly way, and
not as an ascetic achievement, but as signs of God's Kingdom.

God's absolute will cannot be compressed into a law for
this world. It can be set forth only in "signs." Therefore the

demand of Jesus in its deepest meaning does not run: So must thou *act,* but rather, So must thou *be!* What he wants to create is not ascetic or ethical achievements, but men who in word and deed witness to God's Kingdom!

IX

THE OPPOSING FORCES

Jesus' message kept within the frame of Judaism. And yet out of this Judaism grew for him the hostility that brought about his death. On the other hand, in this sentence of death Judaism passed decisive judgment upon itself. For it was not the war with the Romans that left the Jews permanently homeless, but the hostility of the Christians. Such a fateful effect had the opposition between Jesus and the Jews. What did it consist of?

The center of Jesus' message, the announcement of the Kingdom of God, could readily be combined with the Jewish hope. The radicalism of this announcement, however, the exclusive insistence that "one thing is necessary," devalued the claim of all other duties, including the ritual, the legal, and the nationalistic. And Jesus gave expression to this devaluation in his own life: he broke the Sabbath when he felt that God bade him act; he excused his disciples (at least) from the custom of fasting; and the burning national question whether one had really to pay the poll tax to the foreign power of occupation (in Judea and Samaria) he answered in the affirmative, but he viewed it as a secular concern and pointed his questioners to the essential duty, "Give to God what belongs to him." That question had nothing to do with God's Kingdom. In the same way he must have put aside numberless other questions that were viewed as most important by the teachers of his people. And it is precisely because they are laying these burdens on the people and are silent about the essential things, because they "strain out gnats and swallow camels," that he attacks them. "Woe to you Pharisees! You shut up God's Kingdom against men! You do not enter in yourselves, and you keep out those who want to go in" (Matt. 23:13).

A kind of preaching that is concerned so exclusively with what is coming in the future must stand in sharpest contrast to a system that is built on a give-and-take between God and men in the present. To be sure, the strictest representatives of Jewish piety, the Pharisees, also "believed" in the coming Messiah and his Kingdom, but they were not eager for him, for they were satisfied with the present. They believed themselves to be square with God, as the Pharisee voices it in the parable (Luke 18:11). The devaluation of those duties through the principle that "one thing is necessary" must have appeared to them as threatening to undermine and ruin the whole system of piety. Here at the outset there was no mutual understanding.

There was something else besides. Anyone in Judaism who hoped for the coming of the Messiah thought in that connection of a renewal of the nation's splendor; not without good reason was Jesus hailed on his entry with the cry, "Blessed is the coming Kingdom of our father, David!" (Mark 11:10). But Jesus knows otherwise about the fate of this nation. It is like the servant to whom much treasure was entrusted, but who did nothing with it, only buried it (Matt. 25:25). The Jews are like the guests who are invited to the banquet, but regarded something else as more important and so excused themselves (Luke 14:18). With an eye on the nation Jesus speaks of children who sit in the market place but, due to their sheer quarrelsomeness, find no time to play (Matt. 11:16, 17); and he tells a parable of the wicked vinedressers who maltreat the messengers of their lord, and finally kill the son and heir (Mark 12:1–9). And the more clearly Jesus foresees this sort of thing, the greater becomes the cleavage between him and his people.

But the decisive reason for hostility has not yet been touched upon. The strict Jewish piety of Jesus' day rested upon the interpretation of the Bible. Everything had to be derived from the Scriptures, everything had to be proved by them. Jesus occasionally refuted the scribes with a Scripture passage (Mark 12:26), but he did not derive his own message from the Bible. The Law with its precepts could have become for men the occasion for recognizing the absolute will of God. But men have defrauded themselves of this opportunity by their expansion of the precepts into a legal system. As a result, Jesus was now obliged to announce what must obtain in the Kingdom of God, viz., the pure will of God. Therefore in the Sermon on the Mount he put his "but I say unto you" alongside of what "was said to them of old time"; but he did it as the one who himself knew God's will, without deducing it from something else and without any supporting argument. He spoke as one who possessed authority and power, and not like their scribes (Matt. 7:29) — but in the eyes of the Jews that could be viewed only as heresy. For the voices of the prophets were now silent, and no one had the right to announce the will of God on his own account. Consequently the authority that Jesus exercised — no matter what name one gives to it — must be looked upon as blasphemy. Jesus was the archheretic — what need had they of further witness!

To the Jewish authorities the events of the last days of Jesus' life appeared to be a confirmation of this estimate. The Galilean heretic had come with his retinue to Jerusalem for the Passover, the national religious commemoration of the deliverance from Egypt. This was the feast at which all their hopes were annually revived, when throngs of pilgrims, including Galileans, streamed into the city. Throughout the city and in camps outside it were to be found these crowds of pilgrims. The entry of Jesus into the holy city became a triumph, especially through the part taken in it by the pilgrims. Shouts and acclamations of Messianic import were heard. Once in Jerusalem itself, within the sacred Temple area, Jesus came forward as the one who "possessed authority and power." In the outer forecourt sat the dealers selling doves for the sacrifices; there stood the tables of the money-changers, who changed the foreign money and coins of the Roman standard for the old Hebraic or Phoenician money, since it alone was used in the Temple. All these people Jesus expelled from the holy precincts, with words of severe rebuke. He thus not only drew down upon himself the enmity of the persons expelled, but at the same time thereby raised the question as to his authority and its basis; his followers became excited and threatening.

What Jesus himself expected we do not know. But as his journey to Jerusalem has already suggested (see p. 62), so too this public manifestation signifies that he was seeking a decision upon his cause and demanding a decision from the people. His adversaries attempted to unmask him as an enemy either of the Temple or of the Roman government of occupation, in order in one way or the other to obtain a weapon against him. The days of the festival were fast approaching. Jesus must be put out of the way.

It seems that the plan of the Sanhedrin, the Jewish chief council, was to dispose of Jesus before the feast — this is indicated in Mark 14:2. And it also seems that the realization of this plan was actually accomplished just before the feast.

According to Mark 14:2, the Sanhedrin was afraid to wait until the festival for Jesus' arrest. But this is no eyewitness report; instead it is a brief observation, drawing from what actually happened a conclusion as to what had been planned. Whoever put into the mouth of Jesus' opponents the words, " Not during the feast," knew that Jesus had been crucified before the Passover and hence deduced from this the plan of the Jewish council. And the one who wrote thus was not the Evangelist Mark, but another, the author of an older Passion story. We can be sure of this since Mark's own conception of the chronology is quite different.

All the Evangelists have Jesus die on a Friday. But according to the Synoptists this Friday — i.e., the twenty-four hours from Thursday evening to Friday afternoon inclusive — is the first day of the Passover. It is certainly improbable enough that the procurator Pilate would have allowed executions to take place on this high feast day. The Gospel of John likewise (ch. 18:28; see also chs. 19:14; 13:1) gives us clearly to understand, but without further stressing the point, that the first Passover day in that year coincided with the Sabbath. This is not a Johannine correction of other conceptions, for then more emphasis would have been given to the information, but it is a piece of tradition that had come to the Fourth Evangelist just as much other matter also did, especially matter in the Passion story. To the same date points also that decision of the Sanhedrin already mentioned (Mark 14:2), which would not stand at the beginning of the Passion story if it had not actually been carried out. And finally must be included the change made by Mark in the date of the Last Supper and of Jesus' death. It finds expression in Mark only in the short passage, ch. 14:12–16 (not once in the account of the Supper itself); therefore its purpose is merely to make Jesus' Last Supper into a Passover meal and thus bring out the connection between Old Testament rite and Christian sacrament. For all these reasons, preference must be given to the dating that puts the first day of the Passover on the Sabbath, and therefore makes Jesus die on the day before the Passover (see p. 53).

The leaders of the nation intended to do away with Jesus quietly, before the feast, in one swift stroke. Jesus was passing the nights outside the city, in Bethany (Mark 11:11). In the evening he was on the Mount of Olives; festival pilgrims must also have had their camps out there. It would perhaps not be difficult to seize him there in the darkness of the night, without attracting attention; but probably it would be difficult to find him. A guide was needed who was familiar with Jesus' habits, and they found one in the person of Judas. During those days, while Jesus remained in Jerusalem, Judas must have been won over by them for this infamous service.

But as to the reasons for this betrayal, by which Judas' name has come down to after ages as an ignominious symbol of treachery, we know nothing. For the Passion story is not concerned to give reasons for decisions or to describe states of mind; its concern is only to establish faith in Jesus by means of its portrayal of events and to show that "according to the Scripture" things had to happen as they did. To exhibit God's will in the Passion of Jesus is its original intention; its motto is to a certain extent the saying, "The Son of Man goes hence, as it is written of him" (Mark 14: 21). This idea, that the Passion of Jesus fulfilled the Scripture, had already become determinative for the earliest communities and had prompted them, even before there was any story of Jesus' Passion, to read certain passages of the Old Testament as accounts of his suffering and death: e.g., Ps. 22; 31; 69; Isa., ch. 53. In this way the ideas of the Christians

about the suffering of their Lord were formed by the Old
Testament. They were combined with what was already
known, or believed to be known, about these ominous, agonizing hours. That lots were cast for Jesus' garments, beneath
the cross, was read out of Ps. 22:18; it corresponded, however, with a customary practice at executions, and therefore
that it also took place in this case is certainly most probable.
The mockery of the pious by the godless, who " wag their
heads," is the subject of Ps. 22:7. The motive had been incorporated in the Passion story as early as Mark 15:29, where
the words about the head-wagging were quoted; but the
psychological probability of this behavior is so great that no
one will judge this detail to be a mere insertion. The Biblical
saying in Isa. 53:12, " He was reckoned among the transgressors," helped the communities to bear the disgrace of
their Lord's death between robbers (Mark 15:27); but is it
not altogether likely that Pilate, in his short visit to Jerusalem, settled other matters that awaited his decision, and
among them the passing of several death sentences, which
was a duty belonging to his office?

From the Old Testament too the idea may very early have
been gained that Jesus had been deeply agitated and had
complained aloud, and that in this situation he had sought
and found comfort in prayer (Ps. 31:22; 39:12). This conviction also accounts for the words in The Epistle to the Hebrews
that speak of his " strong crying and tears " (Heb. 5:7); on
the other hand, taken in connection with the reported admonition, " Stay awake and pray," it also explains the Gethsemane scene in the Synoptic Gospels. We must not burden
the interpretation of this scene with our own ideas! Here
speaks no neutral observer who, with complete objectivity,
notes that Jesus had for a moment shown signs of weakness.
Here speaks rather a Christian, who recognizes in the cry

of the Lord a confirmation of the divine will as it was revealed in the Old Testament. Not in spite of the fact that he cries out, but because he cries out, Jesus is the one who is fulfilling this divine will. The same holds good of the last utterance (as in Mark and Matthew), "My God, my God, why hast thou forsaken me?" Even this is not the outcry of one overwhelmed with despair, but is the beginning of Ps. 22; and the one who makes this his prayer is certainly not seized with rebellion against God, but is living and dying at peace with God. Either Jesus did actually pray thus, in which case it was not despair but faith that inspired him, or else these words were placed on his lips, in which case the purpose was not to describe his collapse — who among the Christians would have dared to offer such a description! — but to indicate his oneness with God's will.

The Passion narrative is the only long passage in the Gospels that relates events in complete sequence (see p. 33). In this sole instance an effort was made to portray events in succession, since the narrators were thus able to make it plain that the events were to be understood by reference to God's will. And in this case it was possible to relate the full course of things because sufficient material was available. Until the hour in Gethsemane, Jesus had been attended by his entire band. The scene in Gethsemane, of course, no one could really describe; for even the three most intimate disciples had then been overcome by sleep (Mark 14:37, 40). But of the arrest of Jesus the disciples were all witnesses, and the oldest account we possess seems also to appeal to a young man outside the circle of the disciples. He was clad only with a cloak — perhaps because he had been startled out of sleep in the camp of the pilgrims, in the confusion of the attack — and he had followed the crowd. The men who came with Judas seized him by the cloak; he left it in their hands and fled naked. This inglorious episode would not have been told (Mark 14:51, 52) if the young man had not been known to the earliest narrator. The same holds true of the procession to Golgotha. Here Mark and the two other Synoptics tell of an otherwise unknown Cyrenian by the name of Simon, who met the procession and was compelled to bear the cross for the Condemned. What is meant by this is probably the transverse beam on which the offender is first bound and then hoisted up upon a firmly placed pole. But Mark knows also the sons of Simon, Alexander and Rufus (ch. 15:21) — a matter without point for the episode; therefore he or some still earlier narrator must have been acquainted with them. Finally, in Mark 15:40, women are mentioned who had journeyed with Jesus from Galilee and so had been witnesses of the crucifixion; perhaps here too the narrator is indicating how Christian circles obtained information about the death of their Master. Thus while granting the limitations and conditions of our knowledge, we may nevertheless venture to trace the course of events.

On his last evening, Jesus had gathered his disciples together for a supper. Only ceremonial meals were eaten at the beginning of night; the customary hour for the main meal was earlier. If our chronology is correct (see p. 128), then this was not a Passover meal; perhaps it was thought of as an introduction to the feast, as " the Kiddush " (Dedication) — in any case it became a farewell meal. For during the supper Jesus took a flat, round loaf of bread, broke it, as one usually did with bread, and divided the portions of the one loaf among his disciples. In the same way after supper, since goblets with wine were standing on the table, he had one of these goblets passed around among them, and each disciple drank from it. Any man of the ancient world, or any primitive man, would have understood the meaning of such an act even without accompanying words: the disciples were to feel themselves to be a fellowship, just as they had already been while they journeyed, ate, and drank with the Master. For eating together binds the partakers of the meal one to another. However, on this evening, Jesus only distributed, and did not himself partake. And when he said, over the bread, " This is my body," it was not merely a confirmation of the old fellowship, but the founding of a new one; for the words, " This is . . . ," can also mean to a Semite, " This is from now on to be . . ." (see John 19:26). Both the act and the word affirm, accordingly, that the disciples are to remain united as Jesus' fellowship, whether he is personally among them or not. The words that Jesus spoke over the wine have been handed down in more than one form. One has to reckon with the fact that the communities, looking back upon the Lord's death, elucidated this action for themselves. The earliest form of the words, as handed down by Paul (I Cor. 11:25), runs, " This cup is the new covenant [established] in my blood [i.e., by my death]." And, according to Mark 14:25, Jesus added still another saying, " Truly I tell you, I will not again drink of the fruit of the vine until the coming day when I drink it new in God's Kingdom." This utterance likewise points in the same direction as the others: separation from the Master is what confronts this circle, but they are to remain united, even without him, until the day when the table fellowship is renewed in the Kingdom of God. This is his foundation. Even if Jesus had not spoken of his death, he did nevertheless establish this independent fellowship. The Last Supper signifies the founding of the Church.

After the supper, Jesus goes with his disciples out of the

city, over the Brook Kidron, and up the Mount of Olives to
the Garden of Gethsemane. It may well have been his customary evening haunt; perhaps other followers, like that
young man, found him here. In any case, those who came
out to seize him could do so in this spot if someone who
knew about it were to lead them. And it actually happened
that one of the disciples fell so low as to make possible this
sudden stroke, by making known the place and the Man! It
was Judas Iscariot, who had stolen away from the supper. He
now came up to Jesus and greeted him as pupils greeted
their master with the address " Rabbi " and a kiss. Then the
armed band who had surrounded the place knew whom and
whom alone they had to seize. They stepped out of the darkness and took Jesus prisoner. The resistance of a single follower was soon broken. The disciples fled.

The hearing which the court gave Jesus was not reported
to the Christian community, so it appears, by an eyewitness.
According to the Gospels, the prisoner was first brought before the Sanhedrin, presided over by the high priest, and
there his death was decided on. However, though the Jews
had jurisdiction over their own affairs, they did not possess
the right to execute the death penalty, and so Jesus had to be
led before the Roman procurator, who was in Jerusalem for
the festival. But the latter did not need to open a new trial;
instead, he had only to decide whether, according to his
judgment, the punishment should be carried out. And he
decided upon execution! From now on, once more, we know
what many saw, and what many a one like Simon of Cyrene
and the women reported. It is therefore authentic fact that
Jesus was not stoned to death, after the Jewish method, but
was crucified, after the Roman method.

This is reported by all our sources. Some of them know
still more. John tells of a hearing before the old high priest.

Annas, and of a detailed questioning of Jesus by Pilate; Luke, of an ineffectual inquiry by Herod, Jesus' sovereign in Galilee; Matthew, of an intercession for the condemned on the part of Pilate's wife. All four Evangelists, however, unanimously report one feature: Pilate intended to set Jesus free at the festival, i.e., to treat his case as a kind of Passover amnesty. The populace, however, rejected this, and begged amnesty for another prisoner, named Barabbas, who with others had committed murder in an insurrection. That this insurrection had any connection with Jesus' cause is not only incapable of proof but obviously counter to the meaning of the text: opposed to the King of the Kingdom of God must be set a rival, one who is most deeply involved in the world's iniquity. Even though we know nothing of any such amnesty as a custom, there is no reason to doubt the scene; the assumption of invention would mean ascribing to the earliest reporters a plastic propensity and a poetic power such as is not to be observed elsewhere in the narrative.

To be sure, the course of events described by the Evangelists has been doubted on other grounds; for one thing, the Jews at that time still did have the right of execution. The fact that Jesus was crucified, and not stoned to death, proves, moreover, that he was deftly and quickly shifted from the Sanhedrin into the hands of the Romans. Whatever may have been the case as to the Jewish right of execution at that date, the procedure was in any event a hurried trial, corresponding neither to Jewish nor to Roman law. The Christians assumed that a saying of Jesus against the Temple played some part in this, and the outcome proves that Jesus was led to Pilate with the political charge of being a pretender to the throne (see p. 95). Of the disciples only Peter was nearby, but not where he could hear any of the testimony. He had slipped into the courtyard of the palace where the Sanhedrin was assembled — according to John 18:15 he was led in by a Jerusalem follower of Jesus. There, however, the men and women servants found out that he belonged to Jesus; he tried to get out of this by brusquely denying any connection with the prisoner. That Peter — sometime during the night, and before the hour that was called "cock-crow" — was unfaithful to his Lord was acknowledged by the earliest community. Probably the apostle himself, later on, as announcer of the resurrection, found in the vision vouchsafed him the divine forgiveness for his disloyalty, and so related the one fact with the other.

Pilate resided in the palace of Herod on the west side of the city. When the execution had been approved by the procurator, after a hurried examination, soldiers led Jesus and two others consigned to the same fate out of the north gate of the city to the place of execution. The little hill, on which the poles had already been set up, was called, on account of its shape, Golgotha, "a skull." Thus the procession did not go by the route that is shown today as "the way of the cross"; for that assumes that the Castle of Antonia, just north of the Temple on the eastern hill, was the starting point. The crucifixion was introduced, as usual, by a scourging; no wonder that Jesus was so weakened by the journey to the place of execution that Simon of Cyrene had to carry the wooden crossbeam for him. That Jesus' body had already suffered severe injuries is shown also by his quick death. The time from nine o'clock in the forenoon till three in the afternoon is relatively short; for execution on the cross was an agonizing punishment which included long-drawn-out death pangs and was usually ended at last with the fatal spear thrust. Shocks of all kinds might shorten the agony; nails and their marks, however, find their first mention in John. The possibility of a quick hemorrhage seems hardly likely. It was, in the words of Cicero, the worst and most frightful form of the death penalty.

This death in ignominy and shame was soon to be celebrated in adoration by a mighty throng of confessors of Jesus. But when it took place, not the least of his sufferings was the fact that not a single friend was near him. At least none was nearby who as a witness handed on to Jesus' community the memory of his last hours. It would have been natural to fill out these gaps in the Christians' knowledge with elevating and touching traits, and so to provide a legend for the Martyr. This did in fact take place later, and is to be observed most clearly in Luke. A prayer for his enemies, the conversion of a fellow victim, and (in John) concern for his mother — these are the utterances that characterize the Dying One; one may at least say of them that they are worthy of his message and in this sense they are not unfairly placed upon his lips. But the earliest narrative, as preserved by Mark, knows nothing of all this. It contents itself with portraying the picture of the Crucified in a few verses according to the Passion testimonies of the Old Testament, according to Ps. 22 and 69, according to Isa., ch. 53. In so doing it meets — as has been shown already in regard to the motif of the division of his garments — what is historically correct or at least probable. But that is not its primary reason for doing so; instead, it is the certainty that everything had taken place according to the Scripture, i.e., according to God's will, and that Jesus' enemies demonstrated, without knowing it, that God's eternal counsel of salvation was here being fulfilled. Thus his being numbered among the transgressors, as well as his refreshment with a drink (or perhaps it was an attempt to benumb his senses, Mark 15:23), the casting of lots for his garments, and also the mockery of those who passed by — all these details are understood as evidence of the will of

God. And so likewise even the Roman governor himself is
made to preach the Gospel: he has the inscription that was
placed over the crossbeam announce that Jesus is " the King
of the Jews " — the Messiah. And the last word of Jesus is the
cry of prayer with which the classical Passion psalm begins
(and not a cry of despair), " My God, my God, why hast
thou forsaken me? " It proclaims that Jesus died according
to God's will.

The shame of this death is God's will; that is what the oldest form of the Passion story tries to say. No miracle intervenes, and the challenge to Jesus, the Miracle Worker, now
to save himself sinks away as unrelieved mockery. What
Mark relates in the way of accompanying " signs " is intended to impress upon the readers the world-wide significance of this death: darkness covers the earth, a sinister por-
tent befalls the Temple veil, while even the heathen world
in the person of the Roman centurion recognizes the one
who has just died as a Son of God. But these marvels exert no
influence on the course of events (only in Luke is the populace moved, ch. 23:48). They can no longer serve to comfort
the dying Jesus. In utter humiliation and loneliness his life
comes to an end.

X

~~~~~~

FAITH AND UNFAITH

Here ends the life of Jesus, as far as it can be ascertained by historical science, i.e., that public activity which is the subject of this book. Faith, however, goes farther and relates: "They took him down from the cross and laid him in a tomb. But God raised him from the dead. And during the course of many days he appeared to those who had come up with him from Galilee to Jerusalem" (Acts 13:29–31). "Heaven must receive him until the time when all things must return to a fresh beginning" (Acts 3:21).

The conviction that Jesus did not remain dead, that he is now in the presence of God, and that as Son-of-Man-Messiah he will come again — this conviction is older than the Christian Easter stories. For obviously the earliest community in Jerusalem was founded upon this conviction. Without it the assembling of the disciples in the capital city, to which they were strangers, was absolutely unthinkable — not to mention their decision to engage in "Christian" preaching in the holy city of Judaism. What we should have expected is what Tacitus clearly describes (see p. 17) when he speaks of a "momentary weakening" of Jesus' movement following the death of the Master. But of any such weakening the New Testament knows simply nothing.

The different Easter stories which we read in the Gospels do not belong to the oldest stratum of tradition. For one thing, they differ with each Gospel; and this fact is all the more striking in contrast to the Passion narrative, which is more or less uniformly told in all four Gospels (see p. 33). In other words, we find here in the Easter stories the same variety that we saw in the stories of Jesus' birth and infancy (see pp. 41, 50). There is only one narrative that forms an exception: the story of the discovery of the empty tomb by the women (or, as in John, by one woman) is given in all the Gospels in approximate agreement. But this story of the empty tomb is probably no older than the Gospel of Mark. For Mark 16:8 relates that the women fled from the tomb in trembling and astonishment, " and they said nothing to anyone, for they were afraid." Since the Gospel of Mark concludes with this sentence, in the oldest manuscripts, the words naturally imply that hitherto this incident at the grave had been quite unknown.

If, then, the conviction of Jesus' resurrection was not a consequence of the Easter story, how did it originate? We must not overlook the fact that there were certain preconditions at hand. One may point to the Pharisaic belief in the future resurrection of the dead at the time of the great world transformation. Jesus himself, it would be expected, must inaugurate this change. We may also remind ourselves, and probably with even greater reason, of the belief in the Son of Man. If the Son of Man is to come on the clouds of heaven, then Jesus, the Son of Man, must somehow be raised from his obscure, earthly state and exalted to heaven, in order to come from heaven in glory. This sequence of ideas does not, like the Pharisaic, lay stress upon rising from the grave, but upon going to the Father. As a matter of fact one particular line of development of the New Testament Easter faith is thus already sketched out, in distinction from the belief in a resurrection that is only to a kind of glorified earthly existence (compare Luke 24:36–43). This idea of a heavenly assumption is stressed in the Gospel of John when it speaks of the "exaltation" of Jesus and means, with its characteristic *double-entendre,* both his crucifixion and his ascension, or when it refers to his departure to the Father. The same is true in The Epistle to the Hebrews, which emphasizes the doctrine that, following his crucifixion, Jesus as the true High Priest has entered the heavenly sanctuary. In the Gospel of Luke (ch. 24:26), the Risen One himself stresses these ideas, without, however, making use of the title "Son of Man": "Must not the Messiah suffer all these things, in order to enter into his glory?" Hence it appears that the belief in the coming of Jesus with the clouds of heaven presupposes the resurrection as already having taken place — and this belief was implicit, long before, in the title "Son of Man." We may also refer, finally, to the Last Supper. Since by it was established a communion of the disciples with their absent Master, and since Jesus had uttered the hope that in the Kingdom of God he would once more drink of the fruit of the vine — out of this might grow the certainty that he had not remained dead.

But the New Testament narratives also show that, at least in the hour of crisis, the disciples held no such assurance. They fled (Mark 14:50), and gave up Jesus' cause for lost (Luke 24:19–21). Something must have happened in between, which in a short time not only produced a complete reversal of their attitude but also enabled them to engage in renewed activity and to found the primitive Christian community. This "something" is the historical kernel of the Easter faith. How it evolved is nowhere described. Only a few hints and echoes enable us to say anything at all about it. It is clear that Peter, first of all, then the other disciples of Jesus, and then still other followers, including even his

hitherto unbelieving brother James, had visions in which
they saw their departed Master alive and exalted to heavenly
glory.

Our earliest witness, the Apostle Paul, either at the time
of his conversion or of his commission as a missionary (i.e.,
sometime between the years 33 and 45), received the tradition
that Christ " was raised on the third day in accordance with
the Scriptures, and appeared to Cephas, then to the Twelve "
(I Cor. 15:4, 5). This appearance to Cephas (i.e., to Simon
Peter) is also referred to, not described, as the two travelers
to Emmaus return and hear that " the Lord has risen indeed,
and has appeared to Simon" (Luke 24:34). The story in
John, ch. 21, of the appearance of the Risen One beside the
Lake of Gennesaret is evidently a further development of
this old tradition which made Cephas and the Twelve the
earliest witnesses to the resurrection. The apocryphal Gospel
of Peter also seems to have contained a similar story; the
fragment of this Gospel found in Egypt closes with the return of the disciples to the sea after their homeward journey
from Jerusalem. Finally, one may suspect that the predictions in Mark (chs. 14:28; 16:7) that Jesus would " go before " the disciples to Galilee were leading up to nothing
other than these appearances.

In I Cor. 15:6–8, Paul supplements this oldest Easter tradition by mentioning still other appearances: to five hundred
of the brothers, to James, to all the apostles, and finally to
Paul himself, who had thus seen the Lord. The mention of
his own conversion experience shows that Paul does not
think in terms of a return of Jesus to an earthly kind of existence, however glorified, but of a Lord who is exalted to
heaven and who has — for a moment — become visible. He
clearly knows nothing about the story of Jesus' tomb being
found empty. The narrative of the women on Easter morn-

ing of course presupposes a "physical" resurrection of the buried body. And apparently this story had something more to tell Christian believers than was told by the stories of the appearances, since the resurrection was an example of what should take place on the last day: accordingly we find this story of the empty tomb in all four of our Gospels. But on what this tradition is based, we do not know — nor even whether the story of Jesus' burial (Mark 15:42–47) depends upon that of the empty tomb or is an independent tradition.

Nevertheless, still other stories of appearances of the risen Jesus were told; the scene is now Jerusalem (Luke 24:36), now a nearby village (Luke 24:13), now a mountain in Galilee (Matt. 28:16); at one time it is members of the band of twelve disciples who see him, at another time it is others. There is quite obviously no uniform, controlling tradition, but only a variety of traditions; and the more varied they are, so much the more impossible is it to reduce them all to a single legend. These experiences of various followers of Jesus, in different places, evidently resulted in bringing together the earliest Christian community at Jerusalem. They helped to establish the conviction that Jesus' life had not ended in defeat. They opened up before the community the prospect that their Master's career was not yet at an end, that he would come again to complete his work and bring to pass the Reign of God upon earth.

In view of this hope and of its constant deferment through the centuries, the question now finally arises whether or not Jesus was "right," or whether his work rested upon a fundamental and far-reaching error. This question is likewise one that cannot be given a scientific answer, but can be answered only by the decision of faith. But at least the historical sense can mark off the limits within which an answer is possible.

It has often been emphasized in the preceding pages that the proclamation of the coming Kingdom of God was the heart of Jesus' mission. His mighty deeds, even his words, yes, even the fact of his appearing in the course of human history, are all " signs " of the Kingdom of God. The Kingdom is the goal of his prophecy, preparation for it is the substance of his requirements; his proclamation of the pure, unconditional will of God presupposes the coming of the Kingdom of God; the way in which he confronts men with the actuality of God results from the immediate prospect of this heavenly actuality becoming the earthly one.

If the coming of the Kingdom means nothing more than a cosmic revolution, with the sun grown dark and the stars falling in heaven, and with war, apostasy, rebellion upon earth, with the final arrival of the Son of Man on the clouds, and the Last Judgment — if that is all it means, then the preaching of the speedy coming of the Kingdom was indeed a monstrous error. But these " apocalyptic " expectations are nothing more than certain presuppositions which were tied up with the hope of the Kingdom — for that day, inseparably tied up with it. But in the ministry of Jesus these ideas simply do not occupy the foreground. Here the announcement of the Kingdom leads to the attestation of God's sovereignty: his sovereignty in demands upon men, without regard to whether or not they can be met, under human conditions; his sovereignty in promises to men, without regard to any question as to their possibility. The actuality of God, in its full radical seriousness, manifests itself within time only in the form of " signs," and its true sign is the appearance of Jesus.

Here too, error is possible, and here the genuine decision

of faith or of unfaith is required. Only, the decision now is not whether or not those apocalyptic hopes are adequate, but whether or not one recognizes in the radical nature of the Gospel and of the One who proclaimed it the genuine sign of the actuality of God. The man who affirms this will at the same time realize that this actuality is not something in space and time; but he will know that it exists, and he will believe that it must sometime, somehow or other, come to pass — otherwise God would not be ruler of the world and of history. But the man who recognizes in the tradition about Jesus the Christ contained in the New Testament the true " sign " of God will also recognize that this actuality has already begun to come to pass, precisely in the event whose record is the New Testament. Yet it is a human event — and just as surely as this actuality [of God's Reign] exists, so surely has it not yet come to pass. Between the occurrence of its coming and the occurrence of that historical new beginning in " signs " lies the life of post-Christian humanity. This is the meaning of eschatology for *faith;* the believers are in the world as " those who possess nothing, and yet possess all things." More than this is not given even to faith to know! It must content itself with the historical sign of the revelation in Jesus the Christ.

This sign is historical; that is to say, it is a piece of human history, and not an exception somehow lifted outside the course of events. And this fact makes it possible both to doubt and also critically to investigate the story that is told. Doubt, or unbelief, does not consist in a skeptical attitude toward one or more of the things related in the New Testament; for even if the events did not take place just as they are described there, what did take place can nevertheless be God's " sign," and so can the account of it, fragmentary as it may be or burdened with contemporary views and ideas.

Unfaith really consists in a refusal to recognize the event — and the account of it — as a true sign of God's actuality, and then to dedicate one's life to it. Along with this attitude one may of course look upon the Gospels as good, interesting, beautiful, and worth-while books; indeed one may confer upon them, and upon the Man of whom they tell, the highest possible human titles of honor. But none of these high evaluations and appreciations even touch the decisive question of whether or not God here gave a sign. True, God can make himself known in a perfectly dull and impoverished piece of history; and when he does so, and it becomes the medium of God's self-revelation, it takes on a value superior to that of all the most significant events and most interesting details of human history. In every case, and for faith too, it still remains a part of human history, and the accounts of it remain human records — that is to say, fragmentary, incomplete, subject to error, and even, as a consequence of the limitations of human language, not altogether transparent.

As human accounts of human events they are of course proper subjects of research; but research cannot answer any of the questions involving decision — only faith can provide their answer. Yet since faith discovers, in a piece of history, God's own testimony and guarantee, necessity is accordingly laid upon it to set forth this bit of history as clearly and accurately as possible. Moreover, since through faith this bit of history has itself now become a historical factor of undreamed range of influence, everyone who reflects at all upon the history and the destiny of mankind must be concerned with it. For certainly the future destiny of the race depends in large measure upon the way in which the conflict between faith and unfaith develops — taking both words, as heretofore, in their Christian sense — upon the way in which and the time when that conflict is finally decided.

It was upon the basis of the history of Jesus that Judaism once decided its own fate. Then the religious world of the New Testament, which was the product and the result of that history, became a potent factor in the development of the West. The Reformation, the Anglo-Saxon Awakening, Pietism, and many other movements were the appeal from the existing Church to the power of that earliest Christian history. Again and again has come from the story of Jesus the call for decision. And anyone who takes seriously the present struggle over the Christian religion must certainly realize, whether he be friend or foe, that this call is still insistent today!

BIBLIOGRAPHY

Not all the books listed by Dr. Dibelius have been translated. In the place of untranslated works, books in English have been substituted.

I

JESUS IN HISTORY

Adams, David E., *Man of God*. Harper & Brothers, 1941.
Dodd, C. H., *The Apostolic Preaching and Its Developments*. Willett, Clark & Company, 1937.
 History and the Gospel. Charles Scribner's Sons, 1938.
Grant, Frederick C., *The Gospel of the Kingdom*. The Macmillan Company, 1940.
McCown, Chester C., *The Search for the Real Jesus*. Charles Scribner's Sons, 1940.
Mould, Elmer W. K., *The World-View of Jesus*. Harper & Brothers, 1941.
Schweitzer, Albert, *The Quest of the Historical Jesus*. The Macmillan Company, 1948.

II

GOSPEL RESEARCH

Dibelius, Martin, *From Tradition to Gospel*. Translated by B. L. Woolf. Charles Scribner's Sons, 1935.
 The Message of Jesus Christ. Translated by Frederick C. Grant. Charles Scribner's Sons, 1939.
Grant, Frederick C., *The Earliest Gospel*. Abingdon-Cokesbury Press, 1943.

Form Criticism; A New Method of New Testament Research. Including translations of " The Study of the Synoptic Gospels," by Rudolf Bultmann, and " Primitive Christianity in the Light of Gospel Research," by Karl Kundsin. Willett, Clark & Company, 1934.

The Growth of the Gospels. Abingdon-Cokesbury Press, 1933.

Lightfoot, Robert H., *History and Interpretation in the Gospels.* Harper & Brothers, 1935.

Redlich, E. Basil, *Form Criticism: Its Value and Limitations.* Charles Scribner's Sons, 1939.

Richardson, Alan, *The Miracle-Stories of the Gospels.* Harper & Brothers, 1942.

Scott, Ernest F., *The Validity of the Gospel Record.* Charles Scribner's Sons, 1938.

Streeter, Burnett H., *The Four Gospels: A Study of Origins.* 4th edition. The Macmillan Company, 1930.

Taylor, Vincent, *The Formation of the Gospel Tradition.* The Macmillan Company, 1933.

III

THE WORLD OF JESUS

(a) History

Guignebert, Charles, *The Jewish World in the Time of Jesus.* Translated by S. H. Hooke. E. P. Dutton & Company, 1939.

Mathews, Shailer, *A History of New Testament Times in Palestine.* The Macmillan Company, 1910.

Oesterley, W. O. E., *A History of Israel,* Vol. II. Oxford University Press, 1932.

(b) Geography

Dalman, Gustaf, *Sacred Sites and Ways.* Translated by Paul P. Levertoff. The Macmillan Company, 1935.

Smith, George Adam, *The Historical Geography of the Holy Land.* Revised edition. Harper & Brothers, 1932.

Wright, George E., and Filson, Floyd V., *The Westminster Historical Atlas to the Bible.* The Westminster Press, 1945.

(*c*) Religion

Herford, R. Travers, *The Pharisees*. The Macmillan Company, 1924.

    Judaism in the New Testament Period. London: The Lindsey Press, 1928.

Moore, George Foot, *Judaism in the First Centuries of the Christian Era: The Age of the Tannaim*. Harvard University Press, 1927.

Oesterley, W. O. E., Loewe, H., and Rosenthal, E. I. J., *Judaism and Christianity*. The Macmillan Company, 1939.

IV–IX

THE LIFE OF JESUS

Bousset, Wilhelm, *Jesus*. G. P. Putnam's Sons, 1906.

Bultmann, Rudolf, *Jesus and the Word*. Charles Scribner's Sons, 1934.

Cadbury, Henry J., *Jesus: What Manner of Man*. The Macmillan Company, 1947.

Colwell, Ernest C., *An Approach to the Teaching of Jesus*. Abingdon-Cokesbury Press, 1947.

Dibelius, Martin, *The Sermon on the Mount*. Charles Scribner's Sons, 1940.

Goguel, Maurice, *The Life of Jesus*. Translated by Olive Wyon. The Macmillan Company, 1944.

Hoskyns, Edwyn C., and Davey, F. N., *The Riddle of the New Testament*. Ryerson Press, 1936.

Knox, John, *The Man Christ Jesus*. Willett, Clark & Company, 1941.

Otto, Rudolf, *The Kingdom of God and the Son of Man*. Translated by F. V. Filson and B. L. Woolf. Zondervan Publishing House, 1938.

Scott, Ernest F., *The Kingdom of God in the New Testament*. The Macmillan Company, 1931.

Wilder, Amos N., *Eschatology and Ethics in the Teaching of Jesus*. Harper & Brothers, 1939.

Windisch, Hans, *The Meaning of the Sermon on the Mount*. (Forthcoming.)

X
FAITH AND UNFAITH

Burrows, Millar, *An Outline of Biblical Theology*. The Westminster Press, 1946.

Dibelius, Martin, *Gospel Criticism and Christology*. Nicholson & Watson, London, 1935.

Parsons, Ernest W., *The Religion of the New Testament*. Harper & Brothers, 1939.

Rawlinson, A. E. J., *The New Testament Doctrine of the Christ*. Longmans, Green & Company, 1926.

Weiss, Johannes, *The History of Primitive Christianity*, Book I. Edited by Frederick C. Grant. Wilson-Erickson, Inc., 1937.

INDEX OF SUBJECTS

INDEX OF PASSAGES

A. Gospels

Where parallel passages are involved, Mark is given by preference.

B. Other Scripture Passages